SURFACE AT THE POLE

Vice Adm. James Calvert, USN (Ret.)

SURFACE AT THE POLE

The Extraordinary Voyages of the USS *Skate*

NAVAL INSTITUTE PRESS
ANNAPOLIS, MARYLAND

BLUEJACKET BOOKS

Originally published by McGraw-Hill in 1960.
First Bluejacket Books printing, 1996

Library of Congress Cataloging-in-Publication Data

Calvert, James F., 1920 –
    Surface at the Pole : the extraordinary voyages of the USS Skate /
James Calvert.
        p.   cm. — (Bluejacket books)
    Originally published: New York : McGraw-Hill, 1960.
    Includes index.
    ISBN 1-55750-119-X (pbk. : alk. paper)
    1. Skate (Submarine)   2. Arctic regions—Discovery and exploration—
American.   3. North Pole—Discovery and exploration—American.
4. Underwater exploration—Arctic Ocean.   I. Title.   II. Series.
VA65.S56C35   1996
910′.9163′2—dc20   95-46460
                                                             CIP

Printed in the United States of America on acid-free paper

03 02 01 00 99 98 97 96   8 7 6 5 4 3 2 1

LIST OF ILLUSTRATIONS

ACKNOWLEDGMENTS

I am particularly grateful to the editors and staff of the *National Geographic Magazine,* who not only accepted my first effort at writing, but encouraged me to relate the story of the *Skate* voyages in a full-length book. In addition, it is with the courtesy of the *National Geographic* that almost all of the illustrations in this book are reproduced. Many of them appeared in the article I wrote for its July 1959 issue. Within the staff of the Geographic, I would like to thank specifically Dr. Melville B. Grosvenor, Mr. Frederick G. Vosburgh, Mr. Franc Shor, and Mr. Herbert S. Wilburn, Jr., for their help and encouragement.

A special note of gratitude must go to Dr. Vilhjalmur Stefansson and his charming wife Evelyn. Not only did they supply the *Skate* with much useful information on the Arctic, but conversations with Dr. Stefansson at Dartmouth in early 1959 went far to convince me that a submarine, properly handled, could actually break through the winter ice to reach the surface of the polar sea.

Dr. Waldo Lyon of the Navy Electronics Laboratory at San Diego made available to me several documents and a personal correspondence file from which came the material on the *Sennet, Boarfish,* and *Carp,* as well as almost all of the background on the *Nautilus* of Sir Hubert Wilkins. In addition, he furnished much information of use during the *Skate*'s first venture under the polar ice. His presence on board the *Skate* during the second polar voyage was a source of both knowledge and inspiration.

Before his death Sir Hubert Wilkins gave invaluable advice on maneuvering a submarine around and under the ice. His spirit and ideals will be a part of the *Skate*'s heritage as long as she lives.

The Navy's Hydrographic Office, mainly through the good offices of Mr. Walt Wittmann, gave advice and information on the Arctic without which these voyages would not have been possible.

The Navy's Office of History made available documents on the operations of the *Jack,* which were necessary to insure accuracy in relating experiences now dimming in the memory after almost two decades.

Mr. S. J. Wornom, Jr., of the Electric Boat Division of the General Dynamics Corporation gave the original encouragement to me to write about the *Skate,* and has been a valued adviser ever since. He and Mr. John LaPresle made available the diagrams of the *Skate* which appear in this volume.

Thanks are due to Vilhjalmur Stefansson and Captain Edward L. Beach, US Navy, for their kindness in reading the manuscript. The responsibility for any remaining errors is mine.

Finally, while engaged in the training and operation of one of the Navy's first nuclear ships, I received special help and advice from a large number of wise and capable men. I would like to list them all, but must restrict myself to singling out three who did the most to make the *Skate,* her voyages, and this book possible: Rear Admiral Frank T. Watkins, Vice Admiral H. G. Rickover, and Rear Admiral Frederick B. Warder. The Navy gains its strength from young men who pick up the torch from those who have gone before and shown the way. These men, each in a separate and distinct way, have done that for me.

J F C

Mystic, Connecticut

To
Nancy

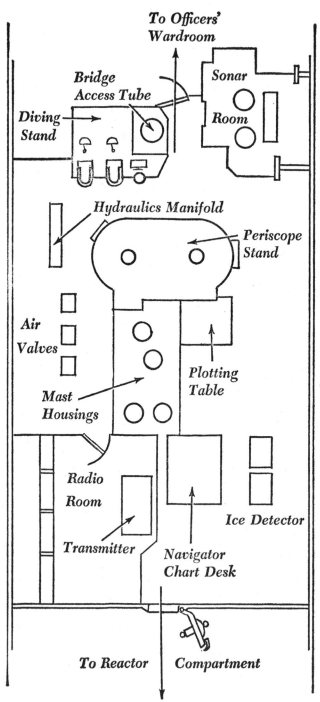

To Officers' Wardroom

Bridge Access Tube

Sonar Room

Diving Stand

Hydraulics Manifold

Periscope Stand

Air Valves

Plotting Table

Mast Housings

Radio Room

Ice Detector

Transmitter

Navigator Chart Desk

To Reactor Compartment

CONTROL CENTER

PART I

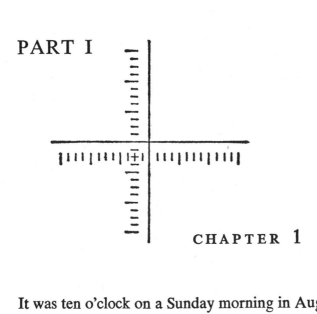

CHAPTER 1

It was ten o'clock on a Sunday morning in August 1958. Around a small table in the center of a long, low, steel-walled room stood a group of four men, gazing intently at a moving pinpoint of light which shone like a glowworm through the glass table-top and the sheet of chart paper that covered it. One of the men followed the path of the light with a black pencil, adding to a web of similar markings already on the paper.

In one corner of this room, some 15 feet away from the group around the table, stood a second knot of men, their eyes fixed on a gray metal box suspended at eye level. Through a glass window on its face was visible the rapid oscillation of a metal stylus, inscribing two compact but irregular patterns of parallel lines across a slowly rolling paper tape. The stylus made a low *whish, whish, whish,* like the sound of a whisk broom on felt, forming a background of noise in the otherwise quiet room.

The pattern on the tape looked like a range of mountains up-side down. One of the men watching it broke the silence. "Heavy

1

ice, ten feet," he said laconically. At the plotting table, the black pencil line continued to follow the path of the moving light.

Then the stylus pattern suddenly converged to a single narrow bar. "Clear water," he called out. This time there was a poorly concealed trace of elation in his voice. At the plotting table, a small red cross was made over the pinpoint of light, completing a roughly rectangular pattern of similar crosses on the paper.

And so the United States nuclear submarine *Skate,* cruising slowly in the depths of the Arctic Ocean, completed preparations in an attempt to find her way to the surface deep within the permanent polar ice pack.

As commander of the submarine, the next move was up to me. I studied the plotting paper closely, the looping black lines that marked the path of the submarine as she reconnoitered beneath the ice, the irregular rectangle of red crosses indicating the spots where the ice ended and open water began. The moving light, showing the position of the submarine on this underwater map, was just entering this rectangle.

"Speed?" I asked tensely.

"One-half knot," came back the answer.

"Depth?"

"One eighty."

"All back one-third," I said, glancing toward the forward end of the room. There two men on heavy leather bucket seats sat before airplanelike control sticks with indented steering wheels mounted on hinged posts. One of these men now reached over and turned two knobs on the high bank of instruments in front of him, conveying my order to the engine room.

A slight quiver ran through the ship as her two 8-foot bronze propellers gently bit the water to bring us to a stop.

I glanced nervously at the plotting paper again. The pinpoint of light was no longer moving.

"Speed zero," said the plotter.

"All stop," I called out. The vibration of the propellers ceased. I stepped up on a low steel platform next to the plotting table. Two bright steel cylinders, 8 inches in diameter and about 4 feet apart, ran from wells cut in this platform up through watertight fittings in the overhead. "Up periscope. I'll have a look."

A slim, crewcut crewman standing next to me reached up and pushed a lever. Hydraulic oil under heavy pressure hissed into the hoisting pistons. One of the steel cylinders began to rise out of its well, moving sluggishly against the pressure of the sea. Small drops of water ran down its shiny barrel from the overhead fitting. Finally the bottom of the cylinder, containing a pair of handles and an eyepiece, appeared from the well, rose to eye level, and sighed to a stop. I folded down the hinged metal handles and put my eye up to the rubber eyepiece of the periscope.

The clarity of the water and the amount of light were startling. At this same depth in the Atlantic the water looks black or at best a dark green, but here the sea was a pale and transparent blue like the lovely tropical waters off the Bahamas. I hooked my arm over the right handle of the periscope and tugged on it. At this depth—where a periscope is normally not used—it pressed heavily against its supporting bearing and could be turned only with great difficulty. A blob of color came into the field of sight. I turned a knob on the periscope barrel to bring it into focus and found we had company. The ethereal, translucent shape of a jellyfish was swimming near the periscope, gracefully waving his rainbow-colored tentacles in the quiet water of a sea whose surface is forever protected from waves by its cover of ice.

I twisted the left handle of the periscope to shift the line of sight upward, in the hope that I could see the edge of the ice. The intensity of the light increased, but I could see nothing but a blurred aquamarine expanse. There was no ice in sight.

"Down periscope," I said, folding the handles up. The crewman handled the hydraulic control carefully to prevent the sea pressure from slamming the periscope into the bottom of the well. I looked around the crowded control center of the submarine. Every face was turned questioningly toward mine.

"Nothing in sight but a jellyfish," I said.

There was a nervous ripple of laughter which quickly disappeared.

"There's a good bit of light here—we must be under some sort of an opening," I went on. I glanced again at the plotting table. The pinpoint of light was resting squarely in the center of the rough rectangle of red marks.

"Do you think we're moving at all?" asked the man who was operating the plotter.

"No way to tell for certain," I answered. "Wait a minute, maybe there is."

"Up periscope." Again the hiss of oil under pressure accompanied the slow upward movement of the smoothly machined periscope barrel. Again I looked out into the icy water. There was our friend the jellyfish. I watched him for almost a minute without being able to detect any movement.

"Down periscope. We're stopped all right," I said, explaining how I knew. "Our jellyfish friend is still looking down our periscope."

There was another faint murmur of nervous laughter, but no breaking the air of tension in the quiet room.

I turned toward the group of men around the ice-detecting instrument. They were gazing intently at the path of the sweeping stylus, apparently paying no attention to anything else.

"How does it look?" I asked.

The man in charge of the group looked impassively in my direction. He held up his left hand with the index finger and thumb forming a circle and the remaining three fingers slightly raised.

Now was the time.

All eyes were on the men at the diving controls of the ship. Behind the two men in the leather bucket seats stood a blue-eyed lieutenant with short-cropped curly hair, the diving officer. He was responsible for holding the *Skate* in its motionless position 180 feet below the surface—a delicate and difficult task in itself. It would be nothing compared to what he would now be called on to do.

With a note of confidence in my voice that I didn't really feel, I said to him: "Bring her up slowly to one hundred feet and stop her there."

Following the intricate commands of the diving officer, a crewman standing by a long bank of control valves started to lighten the ship. The whir of a pump filled the room as sea-water ballast was pumped out of tanks inside the ship. The three-thousand-ton submarine began to drift slowly upward like an enormous balloon. Our depth had been our assurance of safety from collision with the ice; now we were deliberately taking the ship up where danger lay. I noticed with annoyance that my mouth was dry and my heart was beginning to pound. In hope of making out our position as the ship moved upward, I ordered the periscope up again.

"Call out the depths as she comes up—I won't be able to see the gauge," I told the diving officer as I put my face to the eye-piece. There was nothing to be seen but water. Even the jelly-fish was gone, left somewhere below us.

"One forty," chanted the diving officer. This meant the top of the raised periscope, 60 feet higher than the keel, was only 80 feet below the surface—perhaps much less than that from the underside of the ice. I couldn't understand why the ice was not yet visible.

The room was deathly quiet. The whish of the ice detector sounded strangely loud. I walked the periscope around in a complete circle, looking upward and all around. Nothing.

"One twenty." The top of the periscope was only 60 feet below the surface. Suddenly I could see the outline of heavy ice nearby, rafted and twisted ice in huge blocks—and frighten-ingly close. I hastily turned the knob to swing the prism up-ward, but could see nothing but the same blurred aquamarine. I held back an impulse to tell the diving officer to stop right there. I had asked for a gradual ascent to 100 feet, and if I ordered a sudden change it might upset the delicate distribution of ballast which enabled us to rise on an even keel. Already I could hear the noise of water flooding back into the tanks—

the diving officer was preparing to halt the ascent. The thought of what might happen if he could not bring the ship to a stop flashed through my mind.

"Secure flooding," the diving officer said, without moving his eyes away from the depth gauge. The submarine slowed its ascent and stopped at 100 feet as though it had been on a gigantic freight elevator.

I could see the ice more clearly now. The exact distance was difficult to judge, since I had nothing to compare it with. So far as I could see, however, there was no ice directly over the submarine.

But we could only hope we were in the right position. The red checks on the plotting table told us that the lake in the ice we hoped we were under was just large enough to hold us safely if we stayed near its center. The slightest current could carry the *Skate* out from under the opening. Thus, bringing the ship up too slowly could be dangerous, for every bit of delay increased the chance of drifting under the edge of the ice, where the ship could be damaged or destroyed as it rose.

On the other hand, simply to blow the main ballast tanks with high-pressure air and pop to the surface like a cork would be foolhardy. If the thin pressure hull of the *Skate* should then strike the ice it would undoubtedly be ruptured. The ship would be lost with every member of her crew. Such was our dilemma—danger if we came up slowly and even greater danger if we came up rapidly. There was only one thing to do—keep steadily at it, but hold our ascending speed to a rate that would minimize the risk of damage if we collided with the ice.

Of course this depended upon the assumption that the diving officer would be able to maintain the desired rate of rise. A submerged submarine that is not moving forward or aft is like a huge, sluggish balloon. It normally uses its forward motion to control its depth, planing upward or downward by means of control surfaces. Deprived of this motion, the submarine will drift upward or downward depending on the precise condition of its trim and buoyancy. Buoyancy in particular is a very delicate thing—even the temperature and salinity of the sea water can affect it strongly. Here, under the ice, we were staking our ship on the ability of the diving officer to make the *Skate* do something no submarine was ever designed to do—rise straight upward at a predetermined speed.

All of us in the *Skate,* of course, knew that we were engaged in a dangerous business. And there was no doubt that it was easiest of all for me. I was at least in control of the ship and was the only one who could see where we were. The men in the control center knew what was going on, but they had no control over it—they must put their trust in one man and his judgment. The waiting was harder still for the eighty men stationed elsewhere in the *Skate.* They could feel the submarine rising, stopping, rising again—coming ever closer to the ice above. But were we safe? in danger? deeply submerged or close to the surface? They did not know; they could only go about their jobs and wonder—and worry.

A bead of perspiration was starting on my forehead. I looked around the room: every eye was turned in my direction. For better or for worse, I was all they could count on now. No matter what my inner feelings, I must appear as calm and decisive as possible. To do otherwise would not only seriously affect their confidence, it could also imperil the safety of the ship.

I turned to the diving officer: "All right, bring her up, and just let her come out of the water as easily as you can. Call out the depths as you go."

Again the whir of the pump as we carefully lightened the ship. Slowly we began to ascend. I walked the periscope around again, attempting to see if we were moving forward or aft in relation to the ice. There was no apparent movement.

"Ninety feet." The top of the periscope was only 30 feet below the surface.

From here on, we would have to go blind. To keep the periscope up would run too great a risk of having it strike the ice. Even if we were able to avoid the edges of the lake, the danger of hitting a stray floating block was strong in my mind. One of these could bend or shatter our vital and fragile eye, leaving us blind and defeated before we had fairly started. Only a few months earlier, the nuclear submarine *Nautilus* had been at this very same stage in attempting to surface within the polar ice pack. As she neared the surface, a stray block of ice had seriously damaged both her periscopes, and only a superhuman at-sea repair by her fine crew had prevented the abortion of her entire mission.

"Down periscope," I said. Quick as a cat the quartermaster standing beside me pulled the control lever and sent the slender tube hissing downward into the bowels of the ship, downward into safety for its priceless eyesight.

"Eighty feet," chanted the diving officer. The highest immovable part of the ship was now only 30 feet below the surface. We were getting close.

"Seventy feet." The diving officer sounded almost bored with it. How could he be so everlastingly calm?

Without warning, the upward speed of the ship began to accelerate rapidly. I stepped forward, a cry of warning rising to my lips, but checked myself, realizing that everyone in the room knew what was happening. The diving officer was already flooding water into the tanks in an attempt to slow her. It was no use. We had struck a layer of colder or saltier water and were now rising much too swiftly.

"Fifty-five feet," reported the diving officer. There was real concern in his voice. If we were going to hit anything it would be soon. I could not help bracing myself against the shuddering shock that could mean disaster.

But there was no shock. The submarine rose to about 40 feet, hung here momentarily, and sank back to 45 feet.

"Forty-five feet—seems to be hanging there," the diving officer reported, returning to his flat monotone.

Now it would be safe to look. "Up periscope!" The shiny steel cylinder seemed to fly up now, in comparison with its sluggish action in the depths. There was no pressure to hold it back. We were at the surface! I flipped the handles down and swept around quickly.

The light was dazzling. The top of the periscope was in clean, clear, open air! I could see the huge slabs of rafted and broken ice that formed the edges of the lake. The ice seemed dangerously close on all sides, until I forced myself to remember that we are not accustomed to seeing things up close through a periscope— a ship at half a mile seems very close. These slabs of ice, only a few yards away, seemed to be on top of us.

As I twisted the prism downward I could see rippling deep-blue water between us and the ice. My apprehension and fear turned to sheer excitement as I viewed this small blue lake, the jagged ice on its edges, and the icefields stretching as far beyond as I could see. We had come up out of our natural element far below and threaded our way through the treacherous ice to the sunlight above.

But we were not yet on the surface. We were hanging with our keel 45 feet below the surface. Just the periscope and a bit of its supporting structure were out of the water. I carefully measured the distances forward and aft to the ice. It appeared that there would be room to surface the submarine, provided we did not move even a few yards forward or back.

"Stand by to surface!" The words went out on the loudspeaker system, electrifying the rest of the ship. No one outside the control center could know exactly where we were or how we stood until that word was passed. But that order told all: we had gotten our periscope out safely and had found a place large enough to hold the ship.

The team went into action. Valves were opened and closed, switches thrown, reports were made from all parts of the ship to the diving officer. Finally he turned to me and reported: "All vents shut, ready to surface."

I nodded assent, and he turned and ordered: "Blow all ballast!" No need to hesitate now; we could see what we were doing.

The roar of high-pressure air in the ballast tanks was ear-shattering after the strained silence of the past hours. The submarine leaped upward, as though glad to be at least momentarily free of danger from the ice. Yet so skillfully was the job done that the ship moved scarcely a yard ahead or backward.

"Open the hatch!" I shouted to the crewman poised by its locking dogs. He spun the handles and threw the vaultlike hatch open to the fresh air. As we stepped out of it and into the natural atmosphere for the first time in days, I felt the slap of damp, cool air almost as a physical blow. The sky was lightly overcast, and the effect was like that of an unseasonably warm February day in New England, when the temperature hangs just at freezing but seems warm enough to thaw. There was almost no wind.

We climbed quickly to the bridge. The first impression was of being in an infinite desert of ice. On the bridge we were about 25 feet above the water and there was nothing to obstruct our view to the surrounding horizon. There was nothing but a flat patchwork maze of ice floes in every direction. Directly before us the slender black hull of the submarine contrasted with the deep blue of the calm lake water and the stark white of the surrounding ice. The *Skate* was on the surface of the Arctic Ocean deep inside the permanent polar pack. And she was safe. I let out a long sigh that seemed to reach to the bottom of the ship.

My companion, who had been drinking all of this in with me, pointed suddenly downward, near the port side of the ship. There, slowly climbing out of the water and up onto the ice was a full-grown polar bear. He shook himself like a wet dog and gazed curiously at this intruder in his domain. No doubt he was seeing his first atomic submarine!

And, judging from his lack of fear at the sight of the two figures standing on its bridge, it was probably his first sight of man as well.

Courtesy U.S. Navy Hydrographic Office

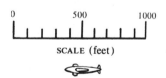

0	500	1000

SCALE (feet)

The polar ice pack in mid-August, photographed from a height of
18,000 feet. The black areas are open water; the small gray spots are
melt ponds. Pressure ridges appear as wrinkles across the floes. The sketch
of the submarine at lower right shows the relative size of the *Skate*.

The bow of the *Skate* nuzzles the edge of an ice floe which is pock-marked with melt ponds and bisected by a narrow lead.

Dave Boyd and Guy Shaffer inspect the lower reactor compartment through a heavily leaded glass window, which shields them from radiation.

Dr. Waldo Lyon scans the ice overhead with the detecting machine which he developed.

Unless otherwise noted, all photographs by the author

James F. Calvert / National Geographic Image Collection

Zane Sandusky adjusts the complex controls
of the inertial navigation system.

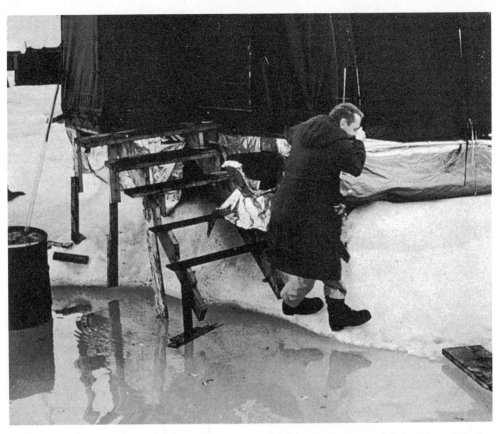

Guy Shaffer negotiates the shaky stairs into a hut at Station Alfa.
Melting of the ice around the huts makes such makeshift ladders necessary.

Major Bilotta's outboard motorboat approaches the *Skate*
from the shore of Station Alfa.

I had come a long way, both figuratively and geographically, to meet this puzzled polar bear at the top of the world. This voyage was for me the climax of three years of hard work and careful preparation. At the beginning I knew very little of the Arctic, and—I must admit—I cared less. Indeed, when my first opportunity appeared to join this program, my plans could hardly have been more different.

In the spring of 1955, I had completed more than two years in my first submarine command, the USS *Trigger,* operating from the large base at New London, Connecticut. I had just received orders to staff duty in Pearl Harbor, and plans for moving to Hawaii were well under way in the Calvert family. My wife, Nancy, and our children were excited about the change and were looking forward to life among the palm trees and pineapples. I was not viewing the assignment with any aversion either.

Then, when only a few days remained until the packers would be coming for our furniture, I received a telephone call asking me to come to the office of Rear Admiral Frank Watkins, boss of all the submarines in the Atlantic Fleet. This is the sort of thing that doesn't happen every day, and I naturally came into his office full of curiosity.

Admiral Watkins is a genial, calm, and enormously capable man in his fifties—one of our top submarine officers. He has been, over the years, a good friend and adviser to me. He didn't keep me in suspense about his summons. He told me that Admiral Rickover wanted to see me in Washington and, if the interview was satisfactory, would want me to go to work for him.

I was thunderstruck. Everyone in New London knew who Admiral Rickover was. At this time the nuclear-powered *Nautilus* had already been operating for several months. The submarine world, of which New London is one of the centers, had been electrified by the spectacular success of this revolutionary ship and by the success of the outspoken, independent officer responsible for getting her built in the face of tremendous obstacles and controversy.

But my mind could hardly adjust to this sudden turn of events. "What does he mean 'come to work for him'?" I asked incredulously. "Doesn't he know I've had orders to Pearl Harbor for months?"

Admiral Watkins is a wise and patient man. "I think he does know that," he said, chuckling quietly, "and I don't think it worries him very much."

"But what would I do?" I asked. "I'm not a specialist in engineering and I don't know anything about nuclear reactors or any of that sort of thing."

Admiral Watkins looked at me steadily and said: "Jim, there's just one thing you know how to do that could interest Rickover—that's command a submarine. I'd advise you to get the next train to Washington."

I did.

The next day was one of those beautiful spring days for which Washington is famous. I walked along tree-shaded Constitution Avenue looking for the address I had been given. When I found it I was certain the address must be wrong. This shabby, gray temporary building couldn't possibly be the headquarters of the famous and powerful man I was looking for. However, a white wooden sign, looking rather temporary and shabby itself, announced that inside were offices of the Atomic Energy Commission.

Inside I found myself in a bare anteroom, where the desk of an attractive Wave ensign effectively barred the path to a set of wooden swinging doors beyond. I announced myself and was asked to sit down and wait.

Wait I did, for perhaps two hours. During this ordeal, my trepidation grew. Not only was Admiral Rickover himself well known; his interviews were also famous. He personally interviewed every person who was a candidate to work for him—not only the engineers and physicists who worked on the designs of his nuclear ships, but even the officers who would take these ships to sea. Even at that relatively early date, stories about the interviews were being told in every submarine wardroom. Many were called, I was told, but few were chosen—and no one ever forgot the experience.

I was prepared for the worst when at last I was escorted through the swinging doors, down a long corridor covered with patched, bilious-brown linoleum, and into Rickover's office.

The Admiral, white-haired and slight of stature, was dressed in civilian clothes. I later discovered that he never wore a uniform if he could possibly avoid it. He shook hands and asked me to sit down. I glanced around his office and saw that it was a place where work went on. A table in the center of the room was covered with reports, documents, letters, and a half-empty cup of coffee. Three sides of the room were lined with heavy-laden bookshelves. There was no carpet on the floor.

"How old are you, Calvert?" the Admiral asked with no preliminaries.

"Thirty-four," I answered.

"Where did you go to school?" he asked.

I described my early schooling at a small Ohio high school and my two years at Oberlin College. Soon we were discussing the subject of my class standing at Annapolis.

"About one hundredth out of a class of six hundred," I said with a bit of pride.

"Why so low?" snapped the Admiral.

While I pondered this unexpected thrust, someone came into the office and handed the Admiral a card. He looked at it with an expressionless face and picked up the telephone on his desk.

The conversation, which moved rapidly, concerned the performance of a company producing material for Rickover's program. The man on the other end of the line was the president of the company. It was all too clear that the Admiral was displeased with the product, the company, and its president. I watched with dismay as the Admiral's voice rose and his face purpled. He stood up, banged his desk until everything on it jumped, and shouted into the phone.

My heart sank. After this outburst I was sure he would either be exhausted or in too bad a humor to carry on an objective interview. The telephone went down with a colossal crash and the Admiral returned his attention to me.

In a perfectly calm voice, with no sign of emotion in his face, he said: "Now why did you say you stood so low at the Naval Academy?"

It was an amazing performance in self-control. From the apparent crescendo of emotion I had just witnessed, the Admiral had returned to complete calm in a matter of seconds. I would have been shaken for an hour after such an argument.

However, I had no time to ponder on this phenomenon. I leaned forward uncomfortably. "Well . . . " I began.

"I'll tell you why," Rickover snapped. "You're either dumb or lazy. Which is it?"

While the Admiral probed mercilessly through the shortcomings of my Naval Academy career, I became aware of one reason why I was doing so poorly. Most of us observe certain routine amenities in our conversation and avoid the abrupt approach to an unpleasant fact. Rickover has trained himself to do just the opposite. He comes directly to the heart of the matter. The more unpleasant it is, the more swiftly he gets to it.

We went on to the subject of spare time and how much reading I got done.

"How many books do you read a month?" he asked.

"About two," I answered truthfully.

"What were the last four?" he asked.

I told him, and he then discussed them with me briefly. It was apparent he had read all four.

"Calvert, do you play golf?" the Admiral asked.

He asked me with the same inflection one would employ to ask a man if he used narcotics.

Sheepishly I admitted that I played occasionally.

"That's fine, just fine," the Admiral said with biting sarcasm. "You admit time is a problem for you in general and yet you go out and waste hours on end playing golf. Tell me, when you go home do you sit and watch the lady wrestlers on television?"

I denied this vigorously.

The Admiral looked at me narrowly. "Do you have a television set at home?"

I admitted hopelessly that we did.

"That's all, thanks," he said, rising with finality.

I walked out of his office a beaten man.

Late that evening I was back in New London.

"It couldn't have gone worse," I told Nancy woefully. "The guy thinks I'm just a golfing playboy."

"You never have any trouble talking to people. What went wrong?" she asked.

"I don't know, the man just overpowers you. You're always off balance in the conversation. Didn't say anything I really wanted to say," I muttered in disgust.

"Well, it probably wasn't as bad as you think," she said consolingly.

"This is one time you're wrong," I said with conviction as I got up to get ready for bed. I was bone-tired from the train trip and the disappointment of the day.

The next morning, as I stepped on board *Trigger,* the duty officer handed me a message from the Navy Department. It read:

ORDERS OF JANUARY 22 CANCELED X WHEN RELIEVED
OF COMMAND OF USS TRIGGER YOU WILL PROCEED TO

WASHINGTON DC AND REPORT TO THE CHIEF OF THE NAVAL
REACTORS BRANCH US ATOMIC ENERGY COMMISSION FOR
DUTY

The message had been sent a few hours after I left Admiral
Rickover's office.

When I reported to the Naval Reactors Branch in May 1955,
the organization was six years old. It was already famous and
had accomplished great things. It was, as much as any government organization can be, built around one man.

In 1946 the heads of the Manhattan Project, which had developed the atomic bomb, turned their attention to peaceful ap-
plications and invited representatives of industry and the Navy
Department to its laboratories at Oak Ridge to work on a project known as the Daniels Power Pile. This project had as its
aim the development of a practical means of producing commercial electric power from a chain-reacting uranium pile.

One of the men who answered the call was Captain H. G.
Rickover, an officer of the regular Navy who was an engineering
specialist. A 1922 graduate of Annapolis, he had served at sea
for many years in a variety of ships, including submarines. During World War II he ran the electrical desk at the Navy's Bureau
of Ships with devastating and often unpopular efficiency.

At Oak Ridge Rickover soon saw that the Daniels Power
Pile project itself was not going to amount to much for reasons
both technical and political. He saw, however, other possibilities
in the newly unleashed force of the atom. Rickover had long
been impressed with the potential importance of the submarine
if it could be freed from its technical limitations. It appeared to
him that atomic power was the key to what he sought. Before
long he was obsessed with the idea of developing a submarine
driven by a uranium pile.

The scientific and political obstacles in the way of this
project were so great that no ordinary man would have considered it seriously. In a way, this was an advantage. During a
few critical years, Rickover had the field to himself.

To start, he had to move back to Washington. When he arrived he had no position, no money, and no authority. All he had was a great idea, ruthless determination, and courage. For eight years he talked, argued, bluffed, schemed, and fought. In January 1955 the world's first nuclear-powered ship went to sea.

Along the way Rickover had done some remarkable things. One of the most important was to create for himself simultaneous positions in the Navy's Bureau of Ships and the Atomic Energy Commission. In both these organizations he was in sole charge of the development of atomic reactors for naval vessels. Only a student of Washington bureaucracy can fully appreciate what an enormous *coup* this was. It was as if Casey Stengel, while remaining manager of the Yankees, had gotten himself installed as president of the American League—with, incidentally, control of all the umpires.

When I arrived in 1955, the *Nautilus* was at sea and the toast of the naval world. The *Seawolf* was ready to be launched at Groton, and new reactor designs for other types of submarines, as well as for a nuclear-powered aircraft carrier and a cruiser, were in the works.

The Navy, as military organizations almost never do in peacetime, had shaken itself free of lethargy and conservatism and struck out in a brave new direction. Its horizons were brighter than they had been in years. Yet the air was heavy with acrimony. Rickover's promotion from captain to admiral had been forced upon the Navy from outside, and resentment against the Admiral's always uncompromising and sometimes unorthodox methods ran deep in Navy circles. After my orders were issued, many officers I had known and admired for years expressed dismay that I was going to Washington to work in Rickover's headquarters. (The skippers of the *Nautilus* and *Seawolf*, Commanders Wilkinson and Laning, had both been trained elsewhere; I was the first line officer to be ordered to work at NRB.)

I found an organization consisting of both civilians and engineering specialist naval officers. I was immediately put under the tutelage of Commander Ed Kintner, a veteran member of

Admiral Rickover's program. Ed, a 1941 Annapolis graduate, is a brilliant engineer. Although he was working six full days a week and was often in the office on Sunday, he devoted much time to my schooling. We started on a review of mathematics, then went on to elementary nuclear physics, and later worked into reactor principles, heat transfer, metallurgy, electrical control, and other technical subjects necessary for a working understanding of nuclear power.

Later Captain Jim Dunford, who had been associated with Rickover since the days of the Daniels Pile, arrived at headquarters. He took over as my tutor when Ed Kintner was transferred to Mare Island as nuclear superintendent at the Navy Yard there. To these men, and to the many civilians—Ted Rockwell, Bob Panoff, Milt Shaw, Ted Iltis, and others—who took time to help me when they were desperately busy with their own work, I shall always be grateful.

To understate the case, Admiral Rickover never mollycoddles anyone who works with him or for him, but there are compensations. I appreciated the fact that he took many long hours of his time to go over with me the things he considered basically important. Often these were not technical matters, nor anything having to do with submarines. They concerned his philosophy of what was ultimately important, for oneself as well as for the organization one worked in.

Perhaps the strongest impression I have of Admiral Rickover is his abiding respect for things of the mind. Not a feigned respect for the sake of reputation, but a genuine fervor which makes him often contemptuous of those who fail to put learning on the same high pedestal he does. His range of knowledge and interest is vast. In the search for competent people for his organization he has interviewed thousands of people, always with heavy emphasis on their educational experiences. From this work he has developed a deep concern about and interest in American education, and his views on this subject are probably as well known as his submarines.

He has tried to instill in all of his subordinates—and I think with some degree of success—a deep respect for the value of time, and a knowledge of the difference between spending it and killing it.

Lastly, he is not afraid. In the world of pulling and hauling for power that is Washington, he does not quail easily. I remember that in his office hung a familiar Shakespeare quote that I would often mull over as I sat waiting for him to finish some interminable telephone conversation:

> Our doubts are traitors,
> And make us lose the good we oft might win
> By fearing to attempt.

Not often did he fear to attempt.

CHAPTER 3

A frequent caller at the Naval Reactors Branch was the skipper of the *Nautilus,* Commander Eugene Wilkinson. He would occasionally drop into my office for a few minutes to see how I was getting along. Dennis (his nickname, in use long before the little fellow of the cartoons came along) is a husky, tall, enormously energetic man. His black hair and sparkling dark eyes seem to underscore the vitality and enthusiasm that mark everything he does.

We had one memorable conversation in 1955. I look back on it as a turning point in my life. We were talking about one of Dennis' favorite subjects, the Arctic Ocean. Dennis does not know how to have a casual conversation. If something is worth talking about, it's worth talking about vigorously.

Leaning forward, Dennis said: "There are only four oceans in the world and this is the one with the most powerful location. Just look where it is." He jabbed a finger at a small chart on my desk.

I understood this well enough. The Arctic Ocean is situated directly between the two heartlands of the world. If there is anything to Admiral Mahan's theories about the strategic importance of oceans, then the Arctic is an area of destiny.

"It's huge," he went on. "Five times the size of the Mediterranean Sea—nearly twice as big as the United States."

"But how about the ice?" I asked. "How much do we know about it? Doesn't it make naval operations more or less impossible?"

"We know more than you'd think," said Dennis. "Some fairly good surveys have been made. And we know the ice thickness averages only about ten feet."

"Where is that—around the edges?" I asked.

"That's the *over-all* average—ten feet," he said with meaningful emphasis.

If that were true, I realized, a submarine would have little trouble operating underneath it. Dennis went on to tell me that the sea ice in the Arctic is made up of flat sections called floes and that these sections butt up against one another with great force, forming pressure ridges that jut both upward and downward.

"How deep do these ridges go?" I asked.

Dennis furrowed his brow and gave me a sidelong look in the way he always does when he is thinking what to say. "Not so much dope on that," he finally admitted. "Probably not more than a hundred feet. But I think we could get under 'em all right!" he said with a grin.

It was obvious he was serious. It was equally obvious he wanted to take the *Nautilus* into the Arctic Ocean under the ice—perhaps as far as the North Pole.

"Sounds pretty wild to me, Dennis," I said, shaking my head. "Suppose you do go up there with the *Nautilus*. What're you going to do when you get two hundred miles inside that pack and something goes wrong? Suppose you have a fire on board? Or a steam leak?"

"That's what the admirals all want to know," said Dennis, flicking his hand as though brushing something aside.

"And how do you convince them there's something to be gained? What good does it do to steam around under the ice? It's spectacular, but what does it accomplish?" I asked.

"You're missing the point of the whole thing," said Dennis with a frown. "This ice pack isn't one solid piece. It's filled with lakes that open and close as the ice floes shift. I've seen pictures of them."

"OK, they're there," I said. "Now how do you get a big submarine like the *Nautilus* up in them? How do you even find them from underneath the ice?"

Dennis grabbed a small chair, spun it around and sat on it

backwards, resting his chin on its back as he looked hard at me.

"Listen, Jim, this isn't a brand-new idea. Men have wanted to take submarines into the Arctic for years. Do you remember Sir Hubert Wilkins? He went up there at least twenty-five years ago in a converted Navy submarine. Had to turn back because the ship gave out. Remember him?"

I thought back to my boyhood the early 30s and could faintly recall the newspaper stories of the expedition. When I had been at the New London Submarine School in 1942, some of the old chiefs teaching there used to tell stories about it.

"I vaguely remember it," I said. "They had a pretty tough time, didn't they?"

"Things have come a long way since then," said Dennis earnestly. "Let me tell you more about it."

American Navy interest in the polar submarine really had its start with Operation Highjump, the huge Antarctic expedition of 1946–47. This venture, first of a long series of postwar Antarctic efforts by the US Navy, was headed by Rear Admiral Richard Byrd and incorporated 4700 men. The Navy wanted, in addition to scientific and geographic data about Antarctica itself, as much information as possible about how its ships would operate in the polar environment. Accordingly, letters were sent around to various Navy commands asking for recommendations, and by an odd set of circumstances a submarine was injected into the plans for Highjump.

During the war, a young physics instructor from UCLA named Waldo Lyon had been doing antisubmarine research for the Navy in San Diego. In the course of the project he became much interested in the possibilities of the very ship his work had been dedicated to defeat. After the war, the Navy Department decided to retain the San Diego experimental laboratory and it was designated the Navy Electronics Laboratory at San Diego. Waldo Lyon remained on the staff.

Not long afterward he saw the letter asking for recommendations concerning Highjump and he convinced the necessary people that something might be learned if a submarine could be made part of the operation.

On the last day of 1946 a strange collection of ships began to penetrate the ice pack of the Ross Sea, the v-shaped notch on the New Zealand side of Antarctica. In the lead was the Coast Guard icebreaker *Northwind,* followed by two large Navy cargo ships and the communication ship *Mount Olympus.* Bringing up the rear, looking forlorn and out of place, was the submarine *Sennet.* And embarked in her, ready to learn whatever he could, was the softspoken but determined Dr. Lyon.

The mission of the main group was to establish an airbase on the edge of the Ross Ice Barrier, the permanent ice shelf that fills the southern end of the Ross Sea. Although it was the middle of the antarctic summer, the ice pack was found to be heavy and extensive. *Northwind* was having her hands full, breaking the way for the three large ships and going back to extract them when they got into difficulties with the ice. As the days went by, it became more and more apparent that the *Sennet,* which was not necessary to the establishment of the airbase, was an impossible extra burden for the icebreaker. Accordingly, *Northwind* turned about and patiently led the wayward submarine back to its more natural surroundings in the open sea. As the *Sennet* left the ice pack her crew looked over the side to see that her formerly gray-painted steel plates had been scraped mirror-bright by the endless action of the pack ice against her sides.

During none of this time had *Sennet* submerged, but Dr. Lyon had learned enough about how her underwater sound equipment acted in the presence of sea ice to start him thinking. It is well that the Navy does not always insist on immediately tangible results when it sends ships to strange and out-of-the-way places. At first it seemed that the voyage of the *Sennet* was a failure and proved nothing, but it had long-term results of extreme importance.

In a few months Waldo Lyon had followed the summertime to the other end of the world and was on the edges of the arctic ice pack in the northern Pacific with the submarine *Boarfish.*

This time a few exploratory dives were made—under the edge of the ice and quickly out again, as a small boy might put his toe in the edge of a cold swimming hole debating whether or not to dive in. But all the time Waldo Lyon was working, trying to develop some sort of gadget that would tell the blinded submarine what sort of ice and how much of it lay overhead.

For this purpose Lyon adapted a conventional machine, the fathometer. A fathometer is normally mounted in the keel of a ship; it sends short dashes of sound energy toward the bottom of the ocean. These echo from the sea floor and are received by an underwater microphone. A timing device, based on the known speed of sound in water, then converts the time delay into distance and a measurement of the depth of the water (a *sounding*) is obtained.

Lyon's idea was to take a fathometer and mount it on the topside of a submarine. Sound would echo from the ice and give its distance above the craft. He found after experimentation that sound would echo from the top as well as the bottom of the ice, thus giving a double echo which could be used to measure the thickness of the ice as well as its distance from the submarine.

Next, Lyon devised a means of printing these time echoes on a traveling paper tape about 8 inches wide. Thus, as the submarine moved along under the ice, a continual cross section or profile of the ice directly overhead would be obtained.

The summer of 1948 found Lyon back in the Arctic, this time with a workable topside fathometer, in the submarine *Carp*. Her captain, Commander Skip Palmer, a southern-accented daredevil of great skill, threaded his way on the surface north of the Bering Strait until he was more than 50 miles inside the ice pack. He did it all alone, benefiting by the experiences of the *Sennet* in the Antarctic. Finding an open lake about a mile in diameter, he submerged the *Carp*, took her under the ice, checked Lyon's experimental ice detector, brought the ship back into the lake, and surfaced her safely. This was the Kitty Hawk of polar submarining.

Dr. Lyon made another arctic voyage, which penetrated as far as historic Banks Island in the Canadian archipelago, but it seemed that his dream of conquering the Arctic Ocean by submarine would never come about. To strike beyond the fringes of the ice pack, an ordinary submarine would have to cruise blindly from lake to lake, hoping to find an opening before its limited storage-battery capacity ran out. A diesel-electric submarine could last only about 30 hours submerged, and then only if it went very slowly—say about 3 knots. This meant it would have about 90 miles in which to locate another opening. Although the odds were in favor of finding one within this distance—at least in summer—the penalty for failure was death. And no responsible submarine commander would ever sign up his crew for this kind of underwater Russian roulette.

So nothing further happened in the field of polar exploration by submarine for several years. Then came a technical development which made the imaginative daydream of yesterday a very real possibility for today. The *Nautilus* went to sea.

Dr. Lyon immediately realized that here was a submarine made to order for his work. A nuclear submarine not only has a virtually unlimited fuel supply, it also needs no air for combustion. Conventional submarines use diesel engines for surface cruising, which require enormous quantities of oxygen, and electric motors when submerged, which run on short-lived batteries. But a nuclear submarine, surfaced or submerged, needs only enough oxygen for the breathing needs of her crew—an infinitesimal amount compared to the vast quantities devoured by combustion engines. Lyon saw that a nuclear submarine could remain submerged under the ice as long as necessary to find suitable openings for surfacing.

Within a short time he was talking to his old friend, Commander Bob McWethy. McWethy, an experienced submarine officer, had long been interested in arctic matters. He had wangled a billet as executive officer of a Navy icebreaker to gain experience in the Arctic and had flown over the ice pack to study the openings in which a submarine might surface. And he had talked to hundreds of officers about the use of submarines in the ice pack, most of whom listened with interest and did nothing. However, when Waldo Lyon began to talk to McWethy about the *Nautilus,* Bob had moved up to a job in the undersea warfare section of the Pentagon, where he was in a position to give more help.

However, there was a lot of resistance to overcome. In 1955 there was only one nuclear-powered ship, and the thought of risking her on some wild escapade left a lot of the Navy's senior officers unenthusiastic. Then Lyon and McWethy went to the heart of the matter: they began to talk to the skipper of the *Nautilus.*

Dennis had already given the possibility a lot of thought. He knew of Lyon's early work in the Pacific and was soon an ardent advocate of a polar probe by the *Nautilus.* This was important, for he, more than anyone else, knew what the ship could or could not do. If he wanted to take her under the arctic ice, people had to listen.

Dennis went at the business of selling *Nautilus*-under-the-ice with his usual vigor. He talked to everyone who could help him and many who could not. When he left my office that summer afternoon in 1955, he had made another convert. Not only was I sure *Nautilus* should go; I also knew, deep in my heart, that I wanted to go myself.

After that conversation my aroused curiosity led me to books on the Arctic to see what I could learn. My reading quickly introduced me to a man named Nansen.

Fridtjof Nansen, born in Norway in 1861, was perhaps the classic arctic explorer. He had read, as did the entire world of the 1880s, of the tragic voyage of the *Jeannette,* a steam-and-sail-powered ship from the United States which attempted to reach the North Pole on the theory that it was high atop a continent, a peninsula of which could be reached by sailing north and west through the Bering Strait. The theory proved tragically wrong. By

September 1879, the year she entered the Arctic, the *Jeannette* was frozen fast in the ice at a comparatively low latitude. She drifted helplessly in the ice for nearly two years, finally to be crushed and sunk. The subsequent tale of hardship and heroism on the part of her crew as they made their way to the Lena River delta of Siberia under the leadership of their captain, Lieutenant Commander George W. De Long, stirred the compassion of the world. Only a few of the *Jeannette*'s men safely made the return to civilization, and they told a tale of horrible suffering and privation. De Long himself perished after arrival on the mainland, before he could reach a village.

There was one aspect of this tragedy which largely escaped the attention of the world but which fired the fertile mind and imagination of Fridtjof Nansen.

The *Jeannette* had sunk near the New Siberian Islands (in the Arctic Ocean, north of Siberia itself) on June 12, 1881. In the autumn of 1884, Nansen read in the Norwegian papers that some of the *Jeannette* wreckage had drifted ashore on Greenland, over 2000 miles from where she had been sunk! What had happened? To Nansen it meant that the ice of the polar sea was on the move. An ocean current must have pushed the ice floes upon which the wreckage was strewn (one of the items was a list of provisions signed by De Long himself) across the Arctic Ocean and out through the Greenland-Spitsbergen Strait.

Here, Nansen thought, was the way to reach the Pole and, more important, to investigate the great unknown regions that surrounded it. He had read in De Long's diary (published by the explorer's widow) that the ice in which the ship was trapped was only 7 to 10 feet thick. Nansen found in this additional evidence that the polar ice was not a frozen and immovable mass, but a covering light enough to be broken and carried along by wind and current. He reasoned that if he could build a ship so strong that it would not be crushed, he could lodge it in the pack near Siberia and allow the drift to carry him all the way to the Atlantic.

Nansen proposed this original plan in 1890 and listened to most arctic authorities ridicule it. He then proceeded to build the *Fram,* as he called his polar ship, sailed it from Norway in the early summer of 1893 through the summer-opened northern passage along the northern coast of Russia, and lodged it according to plan in the ice pack north of the New Siberian Islands. *Fram* was built small and strong, with a rounded hull so that the crushing squeeze of the ice would have a tendency to force her up rather than hold and destroy her. In three years she drifted almost precisely as Nansen had predicted. In the spring of 1896 she broke loose from the ice north of Spitsbergen and arrived triumphantly a few days later in Norway. But Nansen was not on her. He and one of his men had left the *Fram* in March 1895 and attempted to reach the Pole on foot. Food shortage made them turn back before reaching their goal, and it was only after a sledge and kayak voyage that makes a splendid adventure story in itself that they reached the Franz Josef Islands and safety. They were taken by ship from there to Norway, arriving only eight days earlier than *Fram* herself.

Nansen has told this story in his remarkable book, *Farthest North.* It enthralled me, not only because of its exciting narrative, but because the character of the author shone through every page as light through a stained-glass window. Every day he meticulously recorded each piece of data that was of possible scientific use, and he left the impress of his own forceful personality on all his observations and reflections.

To Nansen we owe a great deal of our basic information about the Arctic. He confirmed his hypothesis that the ice floes were not very thick, averaging between 10 and 12 feet thick. Using makeshift sounding equipment, he discovered that the polar basin itself was enormously deep, over 2 miles in some places. He took careful temperature readings and established that the temperature averages about 32 degrees Fahrenheit above zero in summer and about the same number of degrees below zero in winter. He meticulously recorded his observations of the wildlife—the bears, seals, foxes, and gulls who make a permanent home in the frozen regions.

Nansen's observations were accurate, his opinions objective, and his ideals high. If men like him could devote themselves to the Arctic, I thought, then I wanted to do all I could to add to the store of knowledge they had begun.

CHAPTER 4

Not until three years after Dennis Wilkinson first kindled my interest in the Arctic did I get the chance to fulfill what had become a deep desire: to see and explore the icy frontier at the top of the world. My two years of education and labor under Admiral Rickover had been rewarded with the assignment to command the country's third nuclear submarine, the USS *Skate*. And now, in 1958, we were actually on our way. Our destination —the far north, perhaps as far as the Pole and, if things went well enough, even beyond.

Our voyage began—at least superficially—like any other. Both for reasons of schedule and convenience, we slipped our moorings at New London in the quiet of a warm, moonlit July night. A soft breeze, reminiscent more of the tropics than the Arctic, played over the bridge of the *Skate* as we stood down the quiet Thames River toward the open sea. The brightly lighted works of the Electric Boat Division of General Dynamics, where the *Skate* had been launched and completed less than a year before, slid by in the darkness. In a few minutes we were nosing into the dark waters of Long Island Sound.

But the calm of our departure was deceptive, for within, the ship was tense with excitement and anticipation. The whole ship's company of ninety-seven men, plus nine civilians who had volunteered to brave the dangers of the voyage to contribute special technical help, buzzed with speculation. I had not yet divulged all of our orders, but everyone had a general idea of the plans—and that was enough!

As the Connecticut shore receded to an irregular bar of darkness astern, I stood on the open bridge with the officer of the deck, Lieutenant Dave Boyd. Dave is a sandy-haired Scot of rugged appearance and intense energy. He is the sort of trustworthy and capable officer any submarine commander likes to have. For months, Dave had been in charge of obtaining the special equipment that would be needed in the Arctic. He had been making trips to Washington, Philadelphia, and even the West Coast in pursuit of charts, special navigation equipment, special arctic clothing, and other pieces of gear that were either necessary or might prove to be so. He had gathered together books, pamphlets, and training films on the Arctic until his stateroom was bulging and his two roommates threatened him with eviction. With the conscientious zeal and intellectual curiosity typical of him, he had made himself the ship's acknowledged arctic expert, astonishing even the civilian professionals on board with the extent and depth of his knowledge.

That July evening, as we stood on the dark bridge with the sound of the sea whispering along the sides of the ship, Dave's brow was furrowed with concentration. He was reviewing some trouble we had been having during the day.

"Don't like the idea of leaving with one of those ice fathometers acting up," he said, referring to one of our two topside ice-detecting rigs.

"Can't get that cable tight—that it?" I asked.

"Vulcanized it again, but I wouldn't bet much on it," said Dave.

"Could you do anything with it at sea?" I asked, beginning to wonder if we had made a mistake sailing before pinning this thing down more completely.

"Maybe, if we had perfectly smooth water," Dave said, shaking his head.

I didn't ask him about repairs once we got under the ice pack. I knew the answer to that.

"The other one's OK?" I asked, referring to the ice fathometer installed in the top of the sail, the prominent structure amidships that holds the periscopes, radio antennas, and other equipment.

"No trouble so far. I'll check the one that's been giving trouble as soon as we dive," Dave said.

We knew that if the ice detectors were operating properly that, once submerged even though not under ice, we could "read" the surface of the sea with them, could even tell the height and shape of the waves.

We remained on the bridge, silent, as the ship stood out through Block Island Sound and into the Atlantic. As the bow of the *Skate* plowed into the long ocean swells, the silence on the bridge was broken by the clear voice of the radar operator over a loudspeaker: "Contact foxtrot now bears one one zero true, closest point of approach will be one seven five at two miles."

On the horizon, the lights of an approaching merchant ship, still more than 6 miles away, could be dimly seen. The radar operator had indicated that we would come no closer to her than 2 miles. Dave nonetheless studied the lights carefully through his binoculars, then leaned over and spoke over the bridge microphone to the helmsman in the control center. "Come left," he said slowly and distinctly, "to zero nine five."

The bow of the *Skate* swung left and settled on its new course, which would give the merchantman even more passing room.

This extreme wariness against collision is customary in submarines, since the hull is so easily damaged, and the slightest wound is likely to imperil the ship and the lives of her crew. There is almost no such thing as a "slight" accident in a submarine, especially when that accident is a collision. The good submarine officer gives a wide berth to every object which he might run into, or which might run into him.

I could not help thinking, on this balmy night, how our mission in the Arctic would require the very opposite. Our orders directed us to explore the possibility of bringing the *Skate* to the surface in the lakes or leads we hoped to find even in the heart of the ice pack. Instead of giving obstacles a wide berth, we would have to head straight for them. Instead of measuring our margin of safety in miles, we might have to measure in feet. Our

job called for the exercise of more precise judgment, more delicate maneuver, than our duties had ever before demanded.
Could we learn enough, become skillful enough to accomplish
this mission and return in safety? Now that we were actually on
our way, I was not so sure as I had been in the months before.

I prepared to leave the bridge and go below. "When you get
to the thirty-fathom curve," I told Dave, "submerge and set course
for Nantucket Shoals—speed sixteen."

The water would soon be deep enough for the *Skate* to submerge and loaf along at 16 knots, using less power than it took
to make 14 on the surface, where the turbulent drag slowed her
down. We would then proceed south of the famous lightship at
Nantucket Shoals, the last beacon for ships leaving American
waters for Europe—or points farther north.

I descended to the lower bridge, where a watertight hatch led
into the ship. The heavy, open hatch, much like the door to a
bank vault, gleamed dully in the faint light reflected from below.
To me it has always symbolized the private world of the submarine, isolated and self-contained within a hostile element.
Through the eyeports of the lower bridge could be seen the calm,
moonlit Atlantic. Before I saw these friendly waters again—indeed, before I again passed through this hatch, the *Skate* would
have penetrated deep into the frozen Arctic and accomplished
her mission—or failed.

I passed through the hatchway and down a long ladder enclosed in a narrow, watertight steel tube, into the interior of the
ship. I emerged in the middle of the control center, where the
shadowy figures of the half-dozen men on watch could just be
made out in the near-darkness. At night this room is illuminated
only with a few red lights, to preserve the night vision of men
going to the bridge. The two barrels of the periscope shone bale-
fully in the eerie, unreal light. At the diving stand, only the glowing end of a cigarette betrayed the presence of the helmsman as
he steered by the faint red glow of the compass repeater in front
of him, unable to see his course, trusting in the judgment of the
officer on the bridge. A few steps aft a radarman sat silhouetted

before the green fluorescence of his screen, watching contact fox-trot pass about 3 miles to the south of us. A slowly moving, glowing dot indicated its course. Other dots showed the location of more distant ships in our area.

I could not help being struck by the difference between the open bridge and this highly artificial environment where men steered ships without being able to see where they were going and confidently talked about the distance and direction to ships they would never see. This would be our way of life for days, weeks, perhaps even months to come. We would have to trust in the vast emptiness of the sea and derive our sense of direction from instruments which tell us with their electronic eyes, ears, and nerves which way to steer.

I stepped forward into the dark passageway leading to the officers' quarters and made my way more by instinct than vision to the small cubicle which is the captain's cabin.

A built-in bunk, surmounted by a bookcase, a small desk, a chair, a washbasin that folds Pullman-fashion into the wall, a small wardrobe closet, an intercom telephone, and course and depth indicators on the wall—these are its only furnishings. The pastel green color scheme gives only an illusion of airiness and space. Yet one attribute made this Spartan chamber—which would be my home for many days to come—seem like luxury accommodations. The captain's cabin is the only place on board a submarine which has even the semblance of privacy. Indeed, when I got my first command, the conventional (and far less comfortable) submarine *Trigger*, it took me a long time to get used to the loneliness of my quarters.

At the desk I wrote the night orders for the officer of the deck, repeating my order to submerge on reaching the 30-fathom curve, giving the courses to steer, with specific instructions to give all ships a wide berth. I passed the small leather-covered book to the control center, put on my pajamas, and turned in.

I had nearly dozed off when the phone buzzer rang. It was Dave, reporting that he was changing course again to give another New York-bound ship more passing room. I put down the phone without concern. Submarine captains sleep easily when they have officers of the deck like Dave Boyd.

Before long I was awakened by the klaxon blasts of the diving alarm. The *Skate* nosed down slightly as Dave took her under —cautiously because of the still relatively shallow water. I could feel her level off and build up that slight hum of motion that makes her feel like something alive when she puts on speed.

It was good to be on our way.

Next morning,.as is my custom when we are at sea, I took a walk through the ship, visiting every habitable area from bow to stern. I learn all sorts of things on these trips—what shape a lot of the equipment is in, what small problems have arisen or are likely to arise, and (most important of all) what frame of mind the crew is in. I know of no other way for the skipper to get the feel of his ship.

Ever since I have been going to sea in the *Skate* people have been asking me what it is really like to go to sea in a nuclear submarine. I'm always tongue-tied by this question—there is so much to say. But I think the most striking and distinct difference from any other sort of seagoing is that one is free, completely free, from the surface of the sea.

The ancient curse of the seagoer is that strangely nauseating motion imparted to ships by the surface of the sea. For centuries, sailors (especially Navy men) have denied its existence; most would rather choke than admit that it affects them. But it does. Even men who have gone to sea all their lives and have long since gotten over any trace of seasickness, no matter what the weather, know the discomfort and fatigue that come from the surface of the sea. The British have an expressive term for it: *sea-weariness*. And no one knows better what this means than those who take ordinary submarines to sea. Small and low in the water, they are miserable in rough weather and uncomfortable all the time. Forced to remain on or near the surface to get the air which their diesel engines consume in such huge quantities, they are always affected by the motion of the water.

In the *Skate,* however, we are breaking the long-established rules of sea travel. Our throbbing turbines receive their power from a source that has no need of oxygen or any other ingredient of the atmosphere. Traveling 300 feet below the surface day after day, we are almost devoid of any sense of motion. Only the almost imperceptible vibration of our propellers reminds us we are moving. Consequently, to walk through the ship is like passing through a small, highly concentrated, self-sufficient city built deep underground, with mechanical instruments as its only link with the outside world.

Although she is a little shorter than a conventional US diesel submarine, the *Skate* weighs—or, to use the proper naval term, displaces—almost half again as much. The difference is due to the greater hull diameter required to enclose the nuclear machinery. This, of course, allows more roomy and comfortable living conditions than those in conventional submarines. The elimination of the large storage battery and of the reserves of diesel fuel have also increased the space available for the crew.

The *Skate* is divided into two basic parts: the engineering spaces aft, and the control and living spaces forward. The extreme ends of the ship contain the torpedo tubes which are the only armament of the ship (she carries a total of twenty-two torpedoes and the tubes are always kept loaded). Each nest of tubes is serviced by a torpedo room which contains reload torpedoes and also, with characteristic economy of space, bunks and lockers for crewmen.

Almost in the exact center of the submarine is the reactor compartment. Here is located the uranium-packed atomic pile (the reactor) which provides the energy to drive the *Skate* tirelessly through the ocean depths. The reactor consists of a huge jug-shaped steel vessel, almost 20 feet high, containing a gridwork of metal-clad uranium plates. This vessel is filled with ordinary water under pressure so great that it cannot boil.

When control rods which fit into the uranium grid are pulled out to the correct positions, a controlled chain reaction of uranium fission takes place. This reaction generates heat throughout the uranium grid, which is transferred to the water surrounding it. This heated, heavily pressurized water is then circulated out of the reactor vessel, into the large cylinders of the steam generators. Here the pressurized water gives up some of its heat to another water system, at more conventional pressure, on the other side of a metal barrier. This secondary water, as it is called, turns to steam which is carried back to the engine room through heavy steel pipes. Here it spins the turbines which drive the ship and generate electric power for use on board.

The pressurized water, which is pumped in and out of the reactor every few seconds, is of course heavily radioactive. It does not, however, transmit this radioactivity to the secondary water even though it is in close contact with it in the steam generator. This is the key point in the safe operation of the power plant. The steam that goes aft to the engine room is not radioactive, and no special precautions need be taken with it. All of the radioactivity is confined to one compartment, which is safely shielded by lead plates and heavy sheets of polyethylene plastic.

Although no one can be in the compartment when the reactor is operating, this poses no obstacle to passage back and forth through the ship, as a properly shielded walkway is provided. Small round windows of heavy leaded glass are provided so that the crewmen can check conditions in the reactor from time to time.

I began my tour by walking aft through the control center and into the shielded passageway of the reactor compartment. It is necessary for me to stoop my 6 feet 2 slightly as I walk along the 30-foot passageway between the gleaming banks of stainless-steel piping. The reactor is below the floor, the only evidence of its presence a faint hum from the giant centrifugal pumps which circulate pressurized water through the grid of the reactor. The waxlike smell of warm polyethylene filled the air. I stooped to lift the metal cover from one of the inspection windows in the deck of the tunnel-like passageway. Almost 20 feet below me I could see the actual bottom of the well-lighted, deserted reactor-machinery space. All looked in good order; replacing the metal cover, I passed on into the engine room.

Passing several banks of instruments, each as large as an upright piano, I came to the two turbine-generator sets that produce electricity for this city beneath the sea. They are the heart of the ship, manufacturing not only electrical power for lighting, cooking, heating, and air purification, but also the electricity required to control the reactor and to operate the main power plant itself. If these whirring giants should fail us, the *Skate* would soon become a lifeless hulk.

The engine room is lighted in every corner with fluorescent lamps. The gray machinery, black rubber decking, and copper piping combine in a cool abstraction reminiscent of the paintings of Fernand Léger. As I passed, the young men standing by the turbines—probably a little self-conscious in my presence—seemed as efficient and impersonal as the machines they were tending.

I continued aft into the maneuvering room, actually an instrument-filled corner of the engine room which serves as the control center for the power plant. Fred O'Brien, a man of about thirty whose broad face and smiling brown eyes betray his national heritage, sat in front of a panel covered with dials and gauges. One quivering black needle displayed the power level of the nuclear reactor; others showed the temperature of the water passing in and out of the reactor, its pressure, and the velocity of its flow. As O'Brien kept attentive watch on all these meters, he manipulated a small pistol switch that governed the movement of the control rods. With this switch he occasionally ran the reactor rods slowly in or out to control the flow of its power. Next to him sat Wayne Winans, a short, stocky electrician, giving the same close attention to a similar board which contained the meters and controls for *Skate*'s complex electrical system. Beside him, standing over the two steam throttles, one for each propeller shaft, another man stood ready to obey any signal from the control center.

In over-all charge of these men, and of the whole engine room, was Lieutenant Bill Cowhill. He stood back from the control panels so that he could see all of the instruments without moving. Bill is a thin, crewcut young man who seems to exude calm and capability in all directions. His uniform always seems to be pressed, his shoes always shined. He nodded to me as I entered, carefully knocked the ash from his cigarette, and after a glance at the panels before him wrote down several entries in his engineering log in a neat draftsman's hand.

Bill had served with me in my first submarine command, the *Trigger*. He came from Northwestern University, class of 1950, a product of the NROTC program. I well remembered asking him what he had majored in at Northwestern; I was somewhat taken aback to learn that it had been English literature. However it soon became apparent that a knowledge of Shakespeare and Hemingway did not necessarily preclude a lot of knowledge about naval matters. I was particularly happy when, during his tour in the *Trigger*, Bill decided to remain in the Navy as a career officer. Later he was selected for training in nuclear power and graduated second in his class from the Navy's nuclear school at New London.

The maneuvering room is the nerve center for the propulsion plant as the control center forward is for the ship as a whole. When matters are going routinely the maneuvering room is a pretty peaceful place. But when an emergency of any sort occurs —a fire, steam leak, uncontrolled flooding—many things must be done rapidly and accurately in the maneuvering room to prevent serious damage to the power plant and the rest of the ship. It is at this time that the training and presence of mind of men such as these may make the difference between safety and disaster.

Then I thought ahead a few days, visualizing this same group at work in the same space—but with the knowledge that overhead stretched an infinite canopy of ice. Would they be able to work with the same cool efficiency?

I flipped through a metal binder behind Bill Cowhill's shoulder. Here were posted the emergency bills for quick reference in any emergency. The first was fire. Fire is an age-old dread of the seagoer, but it is particularly dangerous to the submarine, with its confined spaces and limited air supply. The menace of heat and flames aside, the atmosphere of a submarine, once fouled by smoke, becomes poisonous to breathe until renewed with fresh air. I noticed the first item on the list of actions to be taken in event of fire: STAND BY TO SURFACE.

I flipped to the next casualty bill: *steam leak.* The engine room of the *Skate* is filled with hundreds of feet of looping, twisting pipe that carry steam to the turbines, to the fresh-water–producing evaporator, and to hissing air ejectors that maintain a vacuum in the condensers which collect the exhaust steam from the turbines. A leak in any of this piping could fill the engine room with billowing clouds of searing steam. The men in the engine room would not have long to live unless the first step on the emergency bill could be executed without delay: STAND BY TO SURFACE.

The next bill was also one peculiar to nuclear submarines— radiation leak. In the event that any of the piping carrying the heavily pressurized water circulating in and out of the reactor should begin to leak, clouds of highly radioactive steam would result, again with dire results unless the ship could be brought to the surface and the air renewed.

The next bill was tabbed with red: *collision.* No newcomer was this one. As long as men have gone under the sea in submarines, they have feared collision. An ordinary egg lowered into the sea can, because of the strength inherent in its shape, go to amazing depths before it shatters from the pressure of the sea. The same egg, however, will fracture if given even the slightest of blows with a sharp implement. A submarine hull is much the same. Constructed to withstand the all-encompassing squeeze of the sea at considerable depths, it will rupture easily when struck by an unyielding object. The internal construction of the submarine is such, moreover, that almost no one has an opportunity to escape. A special alarm is installed in each submarine for only one purpose—to warn of imminent collision. It is a piercing, whining, crescendo that splits the ears and strikes instinctive fear into the marrow of those who hear it.

The history of submarines in all navies over the past fifty years is sprinkled with horror stories originating with collision. On a misty evening in 1925 the American submarine S–51 was lazing along on the surface near Block Island, the same waters *Skate* had traveled as she left New London. Without warning the looming bow of a large merchant ship appeared out of the mist. There was nothing the captain of the S–51 could do. Seconds later the black bow ripped into the tiny sub and sent her careening to the bottom. Only the two or three men on the bridge lived to tell the story.

Two years later, on a stormy gray-clouded afternoon in mid-December 1927, another American submarine, the S–4, was conducting engineering trials near the summer-resort village of Provincetown on Cape Cod. The captain was ready to surface and raised his periscope for a quick sweep around to ensure that all was clear. His face froze in horror and disbelief as he saw the gray sides and foaming bow wave of a destroyer so close that collision was inevitable. A crack like that of an artillery piece echoed through the S–4 as the destroyer's knifelike bow struck her amidships. Heeling at a sickening angle, the submarine plunged to the bottom of Cape Cod Bay as the icy water gushed in. Six men lived for nearly three days in that black tomb on the bottom, tapping signals, but they were never to see the daylight again.

Collision disasters, however, were not restricted to the past. Only a few months before we had left New London, another American submarine, the *Stickleback,* had been conducting training exercises at sea near Pearl Harbor. A mistake in the internal control of the submarine put her near the surface in the path of the speeding escort vessel with whom she was working. The propellers of the surface ship churned the water in a vain effort to stop as her bow sliced into the *Stickleback*'s side. Fortunately the captain of the submarine was able to surface his ship and evacuate it before she plunged to the bottom in water thousands of feet deep.

The *Skate* would be meeting few ships where she was going, nor would she have to run the risks of shallow water in the deep polar sea. But there would be something even more dangerous—ice. Ice can be as hard and unyielding on impact as steel; its edges can stab through the hull of a ship like a sliver of glass slashes paper. At least one famous ship, with far more protection against sinking than we, had been brought to doom by the power of ice. The "unsinkable" *Titanic* had been ripped open and sunk by the submerged spur of an iceberg. No one knew for certain what sharp contact with the ice might do to the eggshell hull of a submarine. No one wanted to find out. At any rate, in the event of submerged collision, the first step was the familiar STAND BY TO SURFACE.

For the submarine in trouble, the surface is synonymous with safety. But there would be no surface for us. Whatever occurred, we would be forced to take care of ourselves inside this all-too-fragile steel-cased bubble of air.

My next stop was the aftermost compartment of the ship, the stern room. At the extreme end are the bank of vaultlike doors of the stern torpedo tubes. Nested on either side of the compartment, interspersed with spare torpedoes, are bunks and lockers for fifteen men. In one forward corner of the room is the ship's laundry, complete with a home-style electric drier. In the other corner is a small laboratory where tests are conducted to ensure that the nuclear reactor is operating properly and that its radioactivity is at a safe level. In the laboratory I saw the ship's medical officer, Lieutenant Dick Arnest, at work "reading" one of the film badges that each member of the crew is required to wear. (The undeveloped film is sensitive to nuclear radiation; the degree to which it turns dark upon development indicates to the doctor how much radiation the wearer has received.) Dr. Arnest keeps records of the total amount of radiation received by each member of the crew. It is interesting to note that the man with the highest recorded amount of radiation has received less than he would in a single set of dental X rays.

It was apparent that *Skate* would find it difficult to shoot any torpedoes from her stern tubes in a hurry. Set up in front of them was a working oceanographic laboratory. Wooden boxes full of empty bottles for water samples were everywhere. On a bench was mounted a spectrometer to measure the index of refraction (ability to bend light) of sea water, and other complicated-looking instruments were all around. In the midst of these gadgets was our senior civilian scientist, oceanographer Dr. Gene LaFond of San Diego. The doctor, a cheerful white-haired man of fifty or so, was to establish himself as an absolutely ruthless poker player at our Saturday afternoon sessions.

Dr. LaFond is also quite a bridge player. He and Mrs. LaFond spent a few years in India, where the doctor taught oceanography. Bridge was a favorite faculty pastime, and the LaFonds were regular participants. The doctor, however, is a man of independent mind and he resented the complete subjection of all the players to one of two bridge systems, each of them invented by men unknown to him. What was more, the players—particularly Dr. LaFond's wife, who was usually his partner—seemed to resent the fact that he was not an adherent of any recognized system. He remedied this lack by writing a bridge book of his own, complete with an elaborate point system and complex rules of play. However, when any given chapter reached the point of concrete advice—what bid to make or what card to play—it was always the same: *Play it by ear.* The book (printed at the Doctor's own expense), was emblazoned *The LaFond System* and was replete with enthusiastic reviews—all written in Hindi.

I left the Doctor adjusting his spectroscope and retraced my steps forward through the engine room and into the forward part of the ship. A conventional submarine is divided laterally into two layers, the lower one of which is normally used for storage. The extra-large hull diameter of *Skate* enables her to be divided into three layers. This creates two living levels and one storage level, with much more space all around. The upper level contains the control center and the officers' wardroom and quarters; the lower level holds the crew's mess hall, bunkroom, galley, and washrooms.

The crew's mess hall is literally never idle. As I entered it, about a dozen of the crew were sitting about reading magazines, playing cards, and studying. The mess hall must serve as a reading room, dining room, study hall, classroom, movie theater, and general lounge for the entire crew of eighty-seven men. It is equipped with its own Coke machine (paper-cup variety) and a hi-fi system which plays either from a juke-box selector or a tape recorder. (The radiomen often tape a news broadcast in the radio room when the ship is at the surface for a few minutes and then bring it to the mess hall where it can be played at leisure.) Just outside the mess hall is located an automatic ice-cream machine. And—of course—in one corner stands a gleaming coffee urn, providing an inexhaustable supply of that essential elixir of Navy life.

I sat down for a moment beside Chief Torpedoman Paul Dornberg, our chief of the boat. He is the man in direct military charge of the crew. The assignment of watches, the assignment of bunks and lockers, the cleanliness of uniforms, the orderliness of the mess hall, the training of new men in the fundamentals of going to sea—all of these are Paul Dornberg's concern. He is well suited for the job. A strapping, vigorous man of about forty, he can be immediately recognized by his luxuriant handlebar mustache. He is also a strict Lutheran, an equally strict teetotaler, and a rabid supporter of the Cleveland Indians.

"Well, Chief," I asked, "have you found a bunk for everyone?"

"Not without looking in all the corners, Captain," Dornberg said. "You know we have better than a hundred people on board with the civilians. Going to have over thirty of them hotbunking—but we didn't promise to bring them *Queen Mary* style!"

Hotbunking is the Navy term for the sharing of a bunk by

two men or, more often, of two bunks by three men. Then, when one of them is on watch, the other two can sleep. It's not the best of arrangements, but it works if everyone cooperates.

I stepped forward into the galley. Walled and equipped in stainless steel, with a white tile deck, this compact room, not more than 12 feet square, contains all the equipment necessary to turn out more than three hundred full meals every day. In addition, the galley prepares sizable snacks for the men who are going on, or just coming off, the night watches. The rest of the night is spent baking for the next day.

In charge of this culinary beehive is a tall cook named Ray Aten. Despite the frequent professional nibbling which sadly tends to expand the girth of Navy cooks, Ray seems to have no trouble staying trim. It may be that the rigors of his job—which he performs most conscientiously and skillfully—help to keep him in fighting shape.

The delightful aroma of roasting pork filled the air. Aten leaned over to look into the ovens and basted one of the browning roasts. They looked as good as they smelled. "For lunch?" I asked.

"Yes, sir, along with mashed potatoes and broccoli," Aten answered with a smile.

Aten has three assistants but they were nowhere in evidence this morning; he was preparing the meal all alone. Due to the smallness of the galley, the cooks take turns with the meals, staying completely out of the affair when it is not theirs. The cook preparing the meal is always assisted by two junior crew members designated mess cooks—the polite Navy designation for kitchen police. The same food is served in the officers' wardroom and the mess hall, so every meal eaten in the *Skate* is prepared in this small room.

The preparation of meals is not the end of Ray Aten's problems, however. Whenever a Navy ship goes to sea there is always the possibility that it will be necessary to keep her there longer than originally planned. For this reason it is Navy policy to carry on board submarines enough food for sixty days, whatever the planned length of the cruise. This meant that Aten had been required to store enough food on board the *Skate* for 18,000 meals when we left New London. This demands more than a little ingenuity.

The third, or lowest, layer in the forward part of the *Skate*'s hull is mainly devoted to this problem. Large shelved rooms hold canned goods, flour, sugar, coffee, and other staples. Other spaces provide cold storage for eggs, butter, vegetables, and fruit, while still others act as deep freezes for meat and frozen foods. The purchasing and proper storage of all this before a cruise—often with very little advance warning—is the sole responsibility of the chief cook.

Aten has one other seemingly minor but absolutely essential responsibility. A ship that travels submerged day after day must have some means of getting rid of its garbage. In the corner of the galley stands a heavy bronze tube about 4 feet high, with a top like that of a pressure cooker. Several times a day garbage and trash are put in nylon mesh bags like ordinary shopping bags. The cooks remove the top from the tube and drop the filled bags into it—it holds about four. The tube reaches all the way to a door in the bottom of the ship. When the top is tightly fastened, the bottom door is opened and the nylon bags are pumped out into the sea. An automatic lock prevents opening both doors at once—an accident that would be fatal to the ship.

The bags must be weighted in order to drop out of the tube properly and to prevent them from floating and thus betraying the submarine's presence in wartime. Bricks are used for this purpose; another of Ray Aten's loading problems is stowing 1000 bricks for the garbage ejector; this is the number of bags of trash and garbage that may be pumped out of the ship on a sixty-day patrol.

I stepped out of the galley, across a narrow passageway, and into the main bunkroom. Here, in a room about 30 feet long and 15 feet wide, are bunks and lockers for forty-one men. This is made possible, with reasonable comfort, by a most efficient use of space. The bunks are in tiers four high. Each bunk is isolated on three sides by sheet-metal barriers, provided with its own ventilation supply, and equipped with an individual reading light. The mattresses and pillows are foam rubber. A small shoe locker is provided at the foot of each bunk, and larger lockers are built into the walls of the room.

At this hour the bunkroom was largely deserted. Only a few men, probably those who had stood the midwatch (midnight to 4 A.M.) were sleeping. A room with this many men living in it is either kept scrupulously neat or it becomes a hopeless shambles. Paul Dornberg sees to it that the first of these two alternatives is followed on the *Skate*. He had, however, made one concession to the storage problems of Ray Aten. The floor of each passageway was completely covered with a single layer of bricks. A cover of plywood had been neatly cut to fit over the bricks, making a smooth and dust-free surface. The ingenuity of submarine sailors in finding storage space is famous, but I had to admit that this went beyond the usual limits.

Closing the bunkroom door (which is lightproof and soundproof to keep out distraction) I walked forward into the *Skate*'s torpedo room. At the far end of the room gleamed the bronze breech doors of the forward torpedo tubes. Along each side were racked the long, cigar-shaped torpedoes. Twenty bunks are strategically located throughout this large room, some of them among the torpedoes.

In charge was Torpedoman Julian Buckley, a fresh-faced, stocky New Englander. He and a group of his assistants were busy with a torpedo which had been pulled into the middle of the room and opened like a giant robot patient on an operating table. Navy philosophy about torpedoes is the same as that concerning food: *Be ready*. No matter what the submarine's mission, a certain number of torpedoes are carried on board. Continual checks are performed to assure that they are in working order. This was what Buckley and his men were doing. Armed with flashlights, tools, and meters, they performed intricate maneuvers deep within the weapon. I doubt that any group of surgeons more earnestly discussed a problem over an open patient, although the language in this case may have been somewhat more colorful.

"Good morning, Captain," Buckley said as he stood up and wiped his brow.

"Good morning. How does this load of fish look—are they in good shape?" I returned.

"Too soon to say, Captain, we've only looked at two of them, but you know how it is—those shops don't take care of them the way they used to."

I smiled, thinking to myself that Buckley, even on one of the world's newest and finest ships, was not immune to the Navy custom of believing that, somehow, things were better in the old days.

"I know you'll have 'em in top shape in a few days," I laughed as I left.

From the forward torpedo room I walked back through the mess hall, up a broad metal stairway (a luxury in place of the narrow ladders usual in submarines) to the control center and into the officers' wardroom. This room serves as combination office, lounge, and dining room, corresponding to the mess hall for the crew. It was now nearly lunch time; a crisp white cloth was on the table, set with shining silver and the plain, blue-trimmed earthenware that has been traditional in Navy wardrooms for over a hundred years.

Our head steward, Woodrow Wilson Jones, was just putting salad on the table and ensuring that everything was in readiness. He then called the officers for lunch; before long we were enjoying delicious roast pork as the *Skate* moved along at 18 knots without noticeable motion, 300 feet below the stormy surface of the Atlantic Ocean.

The *Skate* was a magnificent ship. Everything that human ingenuity and the resources of the nation could provide had been included in her construction. No submariner had ever sailed in such comfort and luxury. Indeed, the ship itself tended to lull one into a sense of complete security—the Arctic and its frozen wastes seemed far outside our world.

And yet, every turn of our propellers brought us nearer our goal. Nearer regions for which the *Skate* had not been designed, regions fraught with danger for this ship upon which our lives depended.

Although none of us on board knew for certain what lay ahead of us, we knew that both the *Skate* and her men were facing the challenge of their lives.

CHAPTER 5

Our second morning out, with eight days still to go before we would reach the edge of the ice, I made my customary visit to the *Skate*'s navigation chart desk, checking on the night's run and examining the track that lay ahead.

Bending over his charts at the desk was our navigator, Lieutenant Commander John Nicholson, executive officer and second-in-command of the *Skate*. A little over 6 feet tall, with broad shoulders, blue eyes, and wavy brown hair, Nick is frequently teased—to his great embarrassment—as being a "Hollywood naval officer." Nick, however, has never needed to get by on his good looks. He was one of the top men in his class at Annapolis and one of the first submarine officers chosen by Rickover for training in nuclear power.

In fact, it was in this connection that I had first gotten to know Nick. Back in 1951, long before the launching of the *Nautilus,* or even the operation of her prototype power plant in the Idaho desert, Rickover had started looking through the submarine force for top-notch submarine officers. His plan was to take four young officers and train them from the ground up, so to speak, in the *Nautilus* power plant.

Rickover informed the Navy Bureau of Personnel (where I was at that time as assistant in the submarine officer assignment section) that he wanted to interview "the two best young submarine officers available" for eventual assignment to the *Nautilus.* Not everyone was anxious to comply with this request, for it was not customary to allow anyone to interview officers personally before assignment. But it was apparently decided that custom did not fit the fiery Captain Rickover, for we were instructed to order two officers in for interview. Since I was a supposed expert on junior submarine officers, the task of nominating the two lucky fellows fell to me.

I made my choices, and before long they appeared in Washington. Soon afterward a phone call blazed its way from Rickover's office to the Chief of the Bureau to the effect that ". . . if those were the two best young submarine officers in the fleet, then I am worried about our future."

To say that this caused consternation in the ranks would be an understatement. Like a tennis ball bouncing down a long flight of stairs the question came echoing down the echelon of command: Who had been responsible for this fiasco?

Considerably shaken, I dragged my feet to the front office with the records (complete since graduation) of the two young officers. I was absolved. It was apparent to everyone that we might have others as good, but scarcely any better.

There followed a long trail of candidates, week after week, all meeting the same fate. Finally, silence. No requests for more submarine officers to be interviewed. Rumors were slyly passed that Rickover was examining the ranks of the naval aviators. Even the Air Force was mentioned.

Then one day Rickover telephoned and said pleasantly that he had liked the looks of the first two boys he had interviewed, and would we have them ordered in as soon as possible, please.

Even in 1951, the men who worked with the wiry nuclear submarine expert admitted that Rickover had little use for the executive who couldn't adjust swiftly to changing circumstances. I was beginning to see what they meant.

One of the two officers was John Nicholson. So far as I know, Admiral Rickover has never had occasion to regret his choice. Now, seven years later, I was glad to see the *Skate*'s most difficult task in Nick's capable hands.

"How was that star fix you got last night?" I asked as I walked up to the chart table.

"Beautiful—worked right out to a point. We're ahead of

schedule, too. That Gulf Stream must be giving us a little help," Nicholson replied with a smile.

As he bent over the charts, the quick and precise way he laid out his track and handled his dividers and pencil bespoke his skill and confidence. He would be needing them both. Navigation is always a troublesome task in a submarine, but navigating the *Skate* under the polar ice would pose problems that, until now, had no solutions.

The basic means of navigation on every ship is still that which took Columbus across the Atlantic—dead reckoning. Dead reckoning is the determination of position by knowing where you have started and then keeping an accurate record of the directions in which you have traveled and the speed at which you have gone. For direction, you must rely upon the compass and its orientation toward north. A log, in essence a water speedometer, provides the necessary information about speed, and with an accurate clock, or chronometer, the distance traveled may be reckoned. The course is then laid out with a pencil track across the chart, and the estimated distance traveled is marked off as the ship moves across the water.

When the ship is at sea and far from landmarks, there are two means of checking the accuracy of your estimated position on the dead reckoning track: celestial navigation and an electronic system called *loran*.

Celestial navigation depends upon the accurate measurement of the angle between some fixed celestial body, such as the sun or a star, and the visible horizon of the earth. Combining this angle with the exact time of the observation the navigator can, with mathematical tables, calculate his position. For centuries this angle has been measured with the sextant, a device that has become a trademark of the mariner. But to use a conventional sextant, Nicholson would have had to surface the *Skate* and go to the bridge. This necessity has been avoided by installing a special device in one of the *Skate*'s periscopes by which the angles of elevation of celestial bodies can be measured with greater ease and efficiency than by any sextant.

Many a dark and stormy night I have watched Nicholson calmly snapping off sights through the periscope as the stars scudded in and out of the clouds. Only the click of the recorder which prints the time and measured angle at the press of a button betrays what is going on. The only trace of the storm is a gentle rock on the *Skate* as she swims along at periscope depth. How different from the old days when on stormy nights the submarine navigator had to brace himself on a swaying bridge, doing his best to shield his sextant from the blowing spray!

The loran system is perhaps even more remarkable for simplicity of operation. The loran measures the minute time difference in the reception of radio signals from towers set up in various locations around the world. These time differences can be interpreted by special tables and charts to show very accurately the position of the receiving ship. For a submarine it is necessary only to expose a buggywhip antenna briefly above water to receive these signals.

These were the tools that navigator Nicholson was using to find the *Skate*'s way as she sped from New London north to Spitsbergen. But what would happen to these tools when the *Skate* ventured under the frozen cover of the Arctic Ocean?

First of all, the loran and periscope-sextant would be unusable. Both depend upon ready access to the surface, however brief or slight. The ice would make this impossible.

Even without these two devices, however, the *Skate* might be navigated reasonably well by dead reckoning, were it not that her compasses would be seriously affected in the far north. Without a correct sense of direction, there can be no dead reckoning.

The *Skate* is equipped with two types of compass. The familiar magnetic compass is attracted to the magnetic North Pole, which is located in Canada more than a thousand miles south of the geographic North Pole. In the Arctic Ocean a magnetic compass doesn't know whether to point south, north, or just give up. Usually it just spins.

The second type of compass is called a gyrocompass, since its essential element is a gyroscope. I'm sure most of us have seen toy gyroscopes spinning off balance in seeming defiance of gravity. They do this because their spinning inertia makes them tend to maintain their position, even against the pull of gravity. It is perhaps not so well known that if a spinning gyroscope is in turn rotated around another axis, its own axis will tend to come to a position parallel with the other axis. The gyrocompass is essentially a gyroscope mounted so that its axis is always level with the surface of the earth, but otherwise free to turn. The earth's rotation causes the gyroscope axis to tend toward a position parallel with the axis of the earth, and thus to point north and south.

However, as the *Skate* traveled northward the velocity of rotation would gradually decrease until at the North Pole it would cease entirely, and the gyrocompass would no longer be able to indicate direction. The effect would, in fact, take place much sooner than that. Compass experts had told us that when we traveled within 500 miles of the Pole our gyrocompass would be wavering and unreliable.

The Arctic Ocean is nearly twice the size of the United States. The prospect of becoming lost under several million square miles of ice did not appeal to any of us. The submarine could easily wander in drunken circles for days without realizing that anything was wrong. Then, when it tried to find its way out from under the ice, it could find itself in an altogether different part of the world than expected if, indeed, it could find its way out at all.

This for a time looked like the Achilles' heel in the project of navigating submarines in the Arctic Ocean. Then, just as nuclear power had made the venture possible in terms of power, another invention of the twentieth century, *inertial navigation*, offered an answer to the problem of finding our way.

One spring day in 1958, a stocky, energetic, and businesslike young man with an engaging smile came on board the *Skate*. He introduced himself as Zane Sandusky, an engineer from North American Aviation. He had been given the job of installing an inertial navigation set in the *Skate*. Furthermore, he said, he was especially interested in doing a good job since he had been informed by his company that he was to go with the *Skate* under the ice to keep the machine running properly!

His assistant, Roger Schmidt, appeared soon after, and the two were quickly accepted as members of the *Skate* crew. Later two regular crew members, William Burns and Charles Mullen, were sent to California to learn the mysteries of inertial navigation. It was the responsibility of these four men to care for the huge electronic marvel that filled half of what had been a fairly good-size bunkroom. It was an impressive sight with its mysterious green-glowing tubes, banks of dials and meters, and rows of flashing dots which, when properly counted, revealed the information stored up in its mechanical brain.

How does it work? Well, gyroscopes are important here too. A series of them stabilize a platform deep in the heart of the system. This platform tends to remain fixed in space—not just in relation to the *Skate* or the earth, but also in relation to the entire universe, to the fixed stars. Delicate devices sense any attempt to move the platform out of its position, whether due to the motion of the *Skate* or the motion of the earth. By sensing, and remembering, the forces that disturb the platform, the system and its computers can determine the position of the *Skate* as she moves about the globe, whether at the equator or under the frozen ice pack at the North Pole.

Naturally the big machine was the butt of a number of jokes on the part of the crew. One day somebody taped a Boy Scout compass on top of the machine, so "it would know which way was north." Another time an Esso road map with the way to the North Pole carefully marked on it found its way into the sanctum of the navigators.

However, we also wanted our conventional gyroscopes to do their best, and we were pleased to have in our group of civilian scientists Clark Ingraham, a topnotch engineer from the Sperry Gyroscope Company. Clark's job was to help us keep our regular gyros running smoothly and to gather data on their performance at high latitudes.

But as I looked over Nicholson's shoulder, I could see the time was drawing near when we would have to find our way mainly by inertial navigation. We were not far from Spitsbergen, the traditional gateway from the Atlantic to the Arctic Ocean.

"I want to make a good landfall here, Nick," I said, pointing at Spitsbergen on the chart before us, "to fix our position accurately before we duck under the ice."

"I'd like to get Wittmann's opinion on the ice boundary before we decide just where to try," he replied. "I'll give him a call."

Soon the lanky form of Walt Wittmann, our ice expert from the Hydrographic Office of the Navy Department, was bent over the chart desk as he sketched his estimate of where we would find the edge of the ice pack. He drew a sweeping line reaching from the eastern shore of Greenland to the northern tip of Spitsbergen.

"That's about it, Captain," Walt said. "Of course, the wind can shift that boundary north or south a good bit."

Nicholson pointed to a long thin island west of the main body of Spitsbergen. "If that's the ice picture, this should be the place to make our landfall—deep water close to the beach and a good radar target with these mountains."

The island Nicholson was pointing at was Prins Karls Forland. Its steep mountains would show up clearly on our radar screen as almost a duplicate of what we could see on the chart—our position would be unmistakable.

I was familiar with Prins Karls Forland. It was just south of Dane's Island, where Nansen's sturdy *Fram* had put in on the fourteenth of August 1896, one day after she had been freed from her three-year imprisonment in the ice pack. Her crew had also used its towering mountains for a landmark.

"Prins Karls it shall be," I said. "Let's head right for it."

I turned to go to my room. A few feet away from the navigator's work table I couldn't help overhearing a couple of crewmen discussing our progress.

On board any ship I'm on, I like to have as little secrecy as possible. I try to give any crew I command as much information as possible about our plans and activities. It was our custom to leave the large ocean chart on top of the work table where everyone could see it, and it was the subject of constant scrutiny and comment.

"Man," I heard a tall torpedoman say as I was about to leave the control center, "we're really roarin' across that ocean! We'll be at the Pole in no time."

"I don't care how fast we go," responded his shipmate, "just as long as we get there first. *Nautilus* had *their* chance. This is *ours!*"

It made my heart turn cold to hear them. For there was one thing I couldn't tell them, much as I wanted to. And since I could not tell them, I dreaded their finding it out.

I went back to my room feeling more depressed than I had for days. It's hard to explain the feeling a submarine skipper has for his crew and their spirit. Perhaps we place more emphasis on morale than necessary, but right or wrong, we are sensitive to it. I honestly believe I can walk through the *Skate* and tell in ten minutes the frame of mind of the crew. And their frame of mind was all too easy to sense. They were—to use the words they would—hot to trot. They had been getting ready to go to the North Pole for almost a year. They had a good ship and it was running well. Nothing lay between them and the North Pole but ocean, and they were experts at eating that up.

People on a ship are fiercely loyal and almost instinctively develop a strong spirit of competition with other ships. The better the crew, the higher their morale, the more they like to compete. Another ship better than the *Skate?* Never heard of it, Mac.

This doesn't imply any animosity or lack of respect for other ships and their crews. A third of *Skate's* officers and many of her enlisted men, for example, had helped put the famous *Nautilus* in commission and had served in her for more than two years before coming to the *Skate.* They knew she was a great ship, and they maintained their friendships with members of her crew. But right now they were in the *Skate,* and they wanted her to be great too. And so the *Nautilus* had become their foremost rival.

This rivalry had come to center about the North Pole. Both ships were involved in Arctic exploration, and the Pole, a target for the ambitions and aspirations of explorers for more than a hundred years, had exerted its fascination on these modern pioneers. The autumn before, the *Nautilus* had reached for the Pole and had been turned back. The *Skate*'s crew hoped this was our chance.

But fate was working against us.

I reached into my safe and pulled out a thin blue-covered folder. It was our operation order for the cruise. I flipped it open.

> When in all respects ready for sea, depart New London and proceed to a point west of Spitsbergen transiting via the Denmark Strait and the Norwegian Sea. When satisfied that conditions are correct, proceed under the arctic ice pack to the vicinity of the North Pole . . .

There was more, but that was the heart of it. A list of missions followed:

> Item 1. Develop techniques for surfacing in pack ice areas . . . all other items are subordinate to this one. . . .
> The military usefulness of an ocean area is dependent on at least periodic access to its surface.

I sighed and put the folder back in my safe. I had practically memorized it. A long story lay behind that small blue folder.

During 1957, while the *Skate* was being built, Nick and I had spent many a long hour speculating on what operations might be planned for the new ship. My thoughts never turned very far from the Arctic. Dennis Wilkinson had finally been successful, and the *Nautilus* was scheduled to make an exploratory trip under the ice in the fall of 1957. Dennis was not going himself, since he had been relieved by Commander Bill Anderson in June of that year, but he was happy to see the *Nautilus* in such good hands for the trip he had fought so hard to bring about.

However, *Skate* would not be ready for sea until wintertime and we knew that arctic operations, if any, would be planned for summer. It would be 1958 before the *Skate* could go. We were not kept long in suspense about the plans for that year, however. Captain Tom Henry, the officer on the Submarine Force staff directly responsible for the nuclear submarines, told us we were scheduled for under-the-ice operations in the summer of 1958—probably to go as far as the Pole!

Although the ship was still building, the crew met this news with wild shouts of approval. From that day onward, every piece of machinery that went into the ship was tested with the question: is this good enough to take under the ice? Every new man who came on board was scrutinized with the idea: is this the sort of man I want to have in a crew that will be required to take the gravest risks ever asked of a peacetime crew?

Believing that the unknown was our worst enemy, I was determined to dispel any apprehensions by relentless education. Training films on the Arctic (mostly for icebreaker ships) appeared. Lectures on polar navigation (as we understood it then) began. Books on arctic survival techniques began to appear.

About this time we learned that the *Nautilus* try for the Pole had not been successful due to compass difficulties (she had no inertial navigation equipment). Our crew shared their feelings of disappointment, but this news also served to make their zeal for the arctic mission all the more keen.

The *Skate* was delivered ahead of schedule and ran beautifully. We had a fine shakedown cruise to Europe, setting transatlantic crossing records in both directions even though the ship was only a few weeks out of the building yard.

Back from Europe and full of enthusiasm I checked on our plans for the coming summer. It was apparent from the minute I walked into Captain Henry's office that things had changed. Captain Henry, who is usually as straightforward as an arrow, was beating around the bush. In addition, he was obviously deeply concerned. "The Washington picture has changed, Jim," he said, "I don't know how we stand for next summer now."

"Is the *Skate*'s arctic cruise canceled?" I asked.

"No, but the *Nautilus* is going now also, and this has changed things," Captain Henry said.

"I don't understand," I said.

"Jim, if I were you I just wouldn't ask any more questions about this. Try to forget it," Henry said.

But it was hard to forget something I'd thought about night and day for months.

A few days later I was talking to Admiral Frederick Warder, who had now replaced Admiral Watkins as commander of Atlantic Fleet submarines. Admiral Warder had known me since 1942, when I first entered the submarine service. I knew that he would tell me what was going on if anyone could.

"Jim, take my advice. There is something going on that I can't tell you about. But you're going to have to lose interest in polar trips. I must ask you not even to talk about it any more," he said.

I swallowed my disappointment as best I could. What hurt most was that I could say nothing to the crew, whose anticipation had reached fever pitch.

A month later I was told about the top-secret transpolar voyage being planned for the *Nautilus*. The *Skate* would also go but would not be first at the Pole. Even then I was one of the few officers in the Navy to know. Again I was cautioned that I could discuss this with no one—not even my executive officer, from whom it was my strict policy to have no secrets.

And so here we were, poised to be the first ship in the history of the world to reach the North Pole, every man in the crew bubbling with zest for the opportunity. It was only right, they said, that *Nautilus* had had the first chance at the Pole last fall. But now: "They had *their* chance. Now it's *ours!*"

This was the albatross about my neck. The aims of the *Skate* cruise were scientific and military. The ability to employ the

Arctic Ocean as an operational area was and is a matter of great military importance to the United States. This was the reason we were being sent. And our exploration of this little-known region could not help but be of scientific value. Whether the *Nautilus* or the *Skate* was first at the Pole was of no real consequence. But that wasn't the view my men had—they were competitors and they wanted to be first. The competitive spirit of submarine crews can accomplish great things. My first three years in submarines were spent making war patrols in the Pacific. It wasn't just desire to wipe the sea clean of Japanese aggression that kept American submarine sailors continually on their mettle. It was the desire to come back to port in Australia or Pearl Harbor with Japanese banners flying and a broom tied to their periscope telling their small world that *their* submarine had made a sweep of a convoy.

And now, there was nothing I could do, nothing I could say, to prepare my crew for their inevitable disappointment.

CHAPTER 6

On the ninth of August 1958, the *Skate* was approaching Prins Karls Forland cautiously from the open sea. A light fog hung over the water, cutting down visibility and completely obscuring the sun. We were beyond the range of any loran station, but both our dead reckoning and our inertial navigation showed us close to our goal. Caution is the word, however, when approaching a rocky coastline in fog after ten days at sea.

Our buggywhip antenna was out of the water, cutting a razor-thin wake in the calm sea as we lazed along at slow speed. A news broadcast was coming in from the BBC. Several receivers in the ship were tuned in as we gathered what we thought might be our last news of the outside world for many days.

The clipped accent of the announcer devoted most of the program to items only of interest in Great Britain. Then:

> The world was thrilled yesterday by news of the incredible feat of the American atomic submarine *Nautilus*. She has crossed from the Pacific to the Atlantic, passing under the North Pole en route. The world-famous submarine is expected. . . .

The rest was drowned out. The word was over the ship in seconds. They knew.

It came at a bad time—hours before we were to go under the ice for the beginning of a test we had prepared a year to meet. But a great weight was lifted from me. Better that they should know now than to think they had been first and learn later that they had not. It was better this way.

It was worse, however, than I had expected. The spirits of

the crew had been as high as the sky; now they were plunged into despair. Over the ship's announcing system I tried to tell them that we must keep in mind the real purpose of the *Skate*'s cruise. We were attempting to demonstrate the military usefulness of an ocean area and the distinction of reaching the Pole first had no bearing on that. We were in the Navy to serve our nation, not to make headlines for the *Skate*.

I'm afraid they didn't hear much of what I had to say. Nevertheless, it is to their everlasting credit that they soon picked themselves up and went on resolutely with the task at hand. In a few minutes Nick appeared with a message he suggested we get off before going under the ice:

TO COMMANDER ANDERSON AND THE MEN OF THE NAUTILUS X HEARTFELT CONGRATULATIONS FROM ALL OF US IN SKATE

I signed the message and told Nick to send it off. I thought that it represented our true feelings beneath our momentary disappointment.

My thoughts wandered to a wintry day in the preceding February when Nick and I had visited the British Museum during the *Skate*'s stopover in England on her shakedown cruise. We came upon an exhibit of several pages from the diary of Robert Falcon Scott, the famous British polar explorer. The impact of seeing the actual pages before me in the glass case made an impression I shall never forget. They were the notes Scott made as he struggled toward his Antarctic base in the face of appalling difficulties—a base he was never to reach. All was recorded in his beautiful and dignified language and firm hand. But as the days went by his handwriting became weaker and weaker, ending with the almost illegible

For God's sake take care of our people.

I do not regard myself as a sentimental man, but I read the last page with blurred eyes that afternoon in London.

Today another page of his diary came back to me even more

vividly. It was written in January 1912 when, after long struggle, Scott and his four companions were at last within striking distance of their aim of many years—the South Pole. Then, over the next rise, they saw the black tents and markers left by Amundsen a few days earlier.

> The Norwegians have forestalled us and are first at the Pole. It is a terrible disappointment and I am very sorry for my loyal companions.... All the daydreams must go....

The best thing to do at a time like this is to keep busy with something important. I intended to do my best.

The *Skate* continued toward Prins Karls Forland until we were in position to try our radar. The radar antenna mast went up and soon green silhouettes on the radar screen were telling us the story we wanted to know. The picture was clearly the stringbean shape of the Forland as shown on the chart. When its direction and distance were measured we knew within a few yards the position of the *Skate*. This sort of navigation—piloting, actually—can only be accomplished within a few miles of land, but it is the most accurate method of all.

There was, as yet, no ice in sight, but we went to a depth of 300 feet and set our course straight for the North Pole, 600 miles away. This was no time to pussyfoot in and out of the ice pack to see how we liked it. In addition, I did not want to remain at periscope depth looking for ice that I might not see until a stray piece bent our periscope over.

As we sped northward our one good topside fathometer—the one in the sail (the other one, about which Dave Boyd had worried the night we left New London, had given out en route to the ice pack)—was pulsing away sending chirping surges of sound up to the surface, feeling for ice. So far, it recorded only open water.

None of us could understand why we were finding no ice. Had a southerly wind blown the pack away from its normal line? Or was it that we did not know what to look for on the ice-detector tape? This did not seem likely, since Rex Rowray, an assistant of Dr. Waldo Lyon, was on board and actually operating the equipment at this time. He had been one of the men who had worked on the early development of the equipment; he knew what to look for. Still, hour after hour went by with no sign of ice.

Finally, I had had enough of this blindman's buff. Shortly after midnight I brought the *Skate* cautiously near the surface and, at very slow speed, poked the periscope above the surface. Just as Rex had said—no ice. Just half-darkness (we were in the latitudes of the midnight sun) and still water. The fog had lifted, and I could see increasingly better as my eye became accustomed to the poor light.

Suddenly, my heart skipped a beat. Stretching across the northern horizon was a dim white line, ominous in the distance. It was the pack.

We submerged back to 300 feet immediately. In a few minutes the ice-detecting machine showed blocks of ice floating by overhead. When a block of ice appeared over the *Skate* the rapidly moving stylus would sketch an exaggerated cross section of the block. Then, when open water again was above the submarine, the stylus would trace a narrow black line. It was fascinating to watch, and Rex soon had a good audience of *Skate* sailors looking at the ice with him—through the magic of the instrument.

As we drove northward at 16 knots, the ice began to grow heavier and closer together. Gradually, there were no more openings. The ice-machine stylus traced the underside of our icy ceiling mile after mile with no interruption by open water. Occasionally it would draw what resembled a huge stalactite as we passed under one of the pressure ridges formed by the grinding together of two floes.

The idle conversation of the men around the machine slowed down and stopped. It had begun to dawn on them that something significant had happened. The inside of the *Skate* felt no different and looked no different but the atmosphere *was* different. An air of tension to which we were unaccustomed began to creep over us. Now, as never before in our lives, we were dependent on the ship.

The control center was lighted only dimly with the red bulbs used at night. This custom, designed to preserve the night vision of the officer using the periscope, was still with us—we had not yet considered that there would be no use for the periscope for some time. In the dim red light the planesmen and helmsman held the ship on her depth and course, expertly and steadily. There was no talking.

The ice machine makes its quiet *whish, whish, whish* from the after part of the room. Up forward the bottom fathometer is being closely watched by navigator Nicholson. We have reached the point where our charts no longer provide accurate soundings. Although the water is deep, Nick watches the fathometer closely. The anguished whine of its ping rings through the control room; back comes the faint echo from the ocean floor 5000 feet below.

In a small room just off the control center still another device, the sonar, sends sound waves quivering out into the dark water. The long purring pulses of this echo-ranging equipment are faintly audible as it probes the water ahead of us, on the lookout for deep pressure ridges hanging down between floes, or —chilling thought—the presence of a deep-draft iceberg.

I walked aft to have a look at the engine room. It was like entering another world. In place of the unearthly red glow of the control center was the harsh white glare of fluorescent lights. In place of eerie electronic noises were the honest whine of turbines and the throbbing grind of gears.

Here the power surged into the propellers to send the *Skate* deeper and deeper into the ice pack. And here stood her young men tending their machinery in matter-of-fact fashion; machinery that used energy stored in uranium atoms before the ice pack was formed—perhaps before the earth itself was created.

CHAPTER 7

Alone in my room I could not fight off the feeling that every turn of our propellers, every spin of the turbines I had just been watching, was taking us farther and farther from safety. How far were we into the pack now? If we had trouble could we make it back to open water before life in this steel tube became impossible?

I told myself firmly to put that sort of thinking out of my mind. Imagination is a great gift, but not at a time like this. But in spite of all my efforts, I had to admit something to myself that I could not admit to anyone else.

I was afraid.

Admitting it, even privately, I felt better. After all, it would take an insensitive clod not to feel some apprehension at a time like this, I told myself. But it was worse than apprehension—it had a depressing grip on my spirit that I could not shake off. The feeling was somehow familiar.

Then I realized what it was. The war. It had been a long time since I had thought of it. On my way out to my first war patrol in 1943 I had felt the same fear. It was the fact that then, as now, I was facing the unknown.

Fear—the ugly child of ignorance and imagination. I was less than a year out of Annapolis, and in my first ship, the submarine *Jack*, bound for the sea area south of Tokyo, already famous as the scene of fierce submarine battles.

A good part of my fear then had been that I personally would not measure up. My task was to operate the torpedo director of the *Jack*. It was my job to translate what the captain saw through the periscope into dial settings to aim the torpedoes. We had practiced interminably against ships at New London and in Hawaii, but dummy practice against friendly ships was one thing. Japanese ships were another. When the chips were really down, I could see myself fumbling. Inept and inexperienced and too young, people would say. How had he ever gotten such an important job?

In the dark, early in the morning of June 26, the issue was closed. The *Jack* made contact with a convoy of five ships leaving Tokyo Bay on their way south. We roared ahead on the surface; as the first glimmer of dawn broke the horizon we submerged ahead of the convoy. At periscope depth Captain Dykers could see the five ships outlined against the pink of the new day. He began to crack out ranges and other information about the ships in the convoy. Automatically I began to crank them into my machine to compute the course and speed of the enemy. A flush came over my face as though an electric heater had been turned on it. I felt faint and trembling.

And then my fear was over. I could see the convoy as clearly as though I had been looking through the periscope myself. Every detail seemed easy. I felt we were master of that sea and the Japanese convoy a toy in our hands.

In a few minutes it was time to shoot.

"Final bearing and shoot," snapped Dykers. "Bearing mark!"

"Set!" I said after putting the number in the machine.

The *Jack* shuddered slightly as the torpedoes raced to their mark a thousand yards away.

Without waiting the half-minute or so it would take those torpedoes to hit, Dykers shifted his aim to the next ship in line. Rapidly he reeled off the new numbers; just as rapidly they went into the machine. We had never worked so quickly.

"Set!" again. Again the slight shudder as the 3000-pound missiles leaped from the bow of the submarine.

No more torpedoes forward. We began to swing the *Jack* to bring her stern torpedo tubes to bear when the entire ocean seemed to start to shake and roar. We were hitting! Those were *our* torpedoes! Up went the periscope. A quick glance showed the two ships sinking. The aiming numbers for the third ship came rattling out.

"Set!" The stern torpedoes were on their way. Now the sound of depth charging began to ring in our ears as a counterpoint to the explosion of our torpedoes. But it was not close—apparently the escort vessel was confused about where the torpedoes were coming from.

Dykers was gleeful. The periscope went up again.

"Take a look at this, Jim," Dykers said and beckoned me to the periscope.

I had been merely an automaton feeding numbers into a machine, making mental calculations, cranking knobs and setting dials, waging an impersonal war of instruments and numbers. Now, through the periscope I saw what the numbers had wrought. A huge gray ship seemed to be standing on her stern with her bow hundreds of feet in the air. I could see a gaping hole as large as a barn in her side. I could see wrecked, tumbled machinery inside that hole. Lifeboats hung vertically from snarled davits. Men scrambled and fell from the sides of the stricken transport. Another sinking ship lay on her side a few hundred yards beyond, belching ugly black smoke and launching lifeboats. I swung the periscope around to the other side. There, not 20 yards away, was a lifeboat of survivors. They looked frightened as they pointed at the periscope; some ducked behind the gunwale of the lifeboat.

I gave the periscope back to the captain. By this time a reload of torpedoes had been completed and we prepared to shoot at one of the remaining ships.

We tracked the ship briefly, obtained the firing values.

"Set!" But before the man on the firing key could press the button, an explosion which made all the other ones we had heard that day sound like popping balloons lifted the stern of the *Jack* almost out of the water.

The airplane escort of the convoy had found us. We had not seen him coming in. Perhaps he had seen the periscope—perhaps the men in the lifeboat had waved notice of our location.

At any rate he had nailed us. I don't know what the explosion must have done to that lifeboat.

The *Jack* scrambled desperately to get underwater again. Then she dove down, down, down, unable to check her descent because her diving planes were jammed by the explosion. We backed our motors in a desperate effort to stop our downward motion. Nothing worked. We went far past the designed diving depth of the submarine. There was nothing I could do to help. The diving officer was doing all he could to unjam the planes, and was blowing the main ballast tanks. I simply stood by my now-useless torpedo-firing machine and watched. I was amazed to find myself so calm when it looked as though the *Jack* were living through her last minutes.

Then the high-pressure air that had been pumped into the ballast tanks began to take effect. The *Jack,* like a wounded animal, slowly began to stop sinking. I looked quickly at the depth gauge and sucked in my breath. I didn't know whether I'd ever again see the men at Groton's Electric Boat Company who had built this much extra strength into the submarine but if I did, I was going to ask them if I could carry their lunch.

The *Jack* was coming up swiftly now—too swiftly. The diving officer opened the vents to release the air entrapped in the tanks to slow her down. But just as she had headed for the bottom, out of control, now she was driving wildly for the surface. She popped out of the water like a cork, in full view again of the plane. He must have been surprised to see us, for we had time to dive again before he dropped his second bomb. But he nearly reached us anyway. It was not as close as the first, but still shattering. I glanced at my precious machine. The glass was cracked, but otherwise it looked all right.

Would it ever shoot another torpedo? I was by no means sure. Around me the radar set had broken loose from its foundation and was tinkling in the middle of the room. The skipper was still holding one of the handles from the periscope—it had broken off in his hand from the impact of the first bomb. Light-bulbs were broken and the glass lay all over the deck. An air line had broken somewhere and air was hissing into the submarine.

But the diving officer had gotten the diving planes working again. The *Jack* came under control about 200 feet below the surface, about where he wanted her.

That, however, was not where Dykers wanted her. "Bring her back to periscope depth," he said. "We're not through shooting yet."

But there was no more shooting that day. At periscope depth we found the attack periscope flooded, the torpedo tubes damaged, and the diving planes still erratic. But most conclusive, the one remaining transport of the convoy, along with the escort, was three miles away and going for all she could make. The airplane was gone, either having run out of bombs or figuring that the obviously stricken submarine was a sure kill. (After the war we learned the latter was the case.)

This had been a rousing introduction to the war. There were tight spots later, but I always had the feeling that we had been about as far as you go and live to tell about it, and so there was no point in worrying. The unknown had been removed.

My reverie ended with a start. It was nearly morning. How long had I been sitting there? It had been years since I had thought about that patrol—I had never before recalled it in such detail.

But there was a difference. In the *Jack* I had been a young fellow, with the swashbuckling Dykers to look to in time of trouble. He seemed to lead a charmed life, and I could never believe that the enemy would ever get him.

Here in the *Skate*, I had to be the one. Whatever my doubts and fears I might acknowledge to myself alone in my room, I could never let them be expressed or shown outside. I might do so inadvertently, but I had to do my best to appear confident and assured.

And, as the younger people lean on the captain, he, in turn leans on them, although they may not know it. What a blessing it was, I thought, to have men like Nicholson on board. With him I could share my burden, even though neither of us would ever discuss it directly. I stepped out into the control center and saw him working over his chart table.

"Nick," I said, "I'm going to turn in for a while. Will you keep an eye on things?"

I was up four hours later and went into the control center to see how things were going. The *Skate* had been driving straight north at 16 knots; we were more than 100 miles within the ice. Whatever befell us now, we would have to deal with it inside the pack. There could be no running for the edge.

I watched the ice machine as it steadily drew the profile of the canopy over us. Occasionally the stylus would trace the thin black line near the top of the tape that indicated we had passed under a stretch of open water—a lake. Then the line would plunge downward to begin the picture of the next ice floe. At 16 knots, the *Skate* was moving more than 500 yards a minute. If a single black line should remain on the trace for a minute or longer we would know we had passed a lake—or a part of one—at least 500 yards long. We hoped this might be large enough for our purpose.

Our ice expert Walt Wittmann had explained the origin of the lakes to us. The winds and currents of the Arctic Ocean exert considerable force on the crust of ice that covers the sea. The crust is broken up into floes (some several miles in diameter) which push and jostle against each other endlessly.

However, this pushing and jostling is a slow process. Sometimes it takes hours for the implacable pressure of millions of tons of ice to form a pressure ridge between floes. Walt told of standing on the ice pack on one occasion watching a pressure ridge form slowly but inexorably although no wind or current was apparent. Pressure had been transmitted across miles of ice floes to be concentrated at this one point where deformation occurred. The opposite can happen as well. Floes just as mysteriously pull apart, leaving lakes of open water sparkling among the fields of ice.

In *Farthest North* Nansen describes how he once walked away from the icebound *Fram* for a distance and found a stretch of open water where ice had been only a few hours before. There was no sun, but it was a time of bright moonlight. "It was strange once more to see the moonlight playing on the coal-black waves," Nansen wrote. "I saw from a high hummock that this opening stretched north as far as the eye could reach."

Although *lake* is probably the simplest word to describe these openings that pockmark the polar sea, it is not the one that Walt used. He divided the openings into two basic groups: (1) Long cracks called *leads,* which appear between floes at all seasons of the year; and (2) lakelike areas of irregularly round or rectangular shape, which usually develop from leads and are especially characteristic of the summer Arctic. Walt called this type of opening a *polynya.* This word is borrowed from Russian and means, loosely, a water opening in the ice.

This word was a jawbreaker for us at first, but if you put the accent on the second syllable and pronounce it to rhyme with *sheen,* you come out pretty well. The over-all result should sound like pull–*een*–yuh. (If you have learned to pronounce this word you are on your way to becoming an arctic expert; it is one of the first requirements. Most people try to accent the second y, and the results are dreadful.) The plural of the word is polynyas, to the great discouragement of people who know Russian.

Polynyas tend to develop more often in the summer, due to the higher temperature. Nansen found that the average summertime temperature through the heart of the Arctic was 32 degrees Fahrenheit. During this period the open water of the leads has no tendency to refreeze and, unless reclosed by the movement of the floes, will remain open. Often a polynya may fill up at its extreme ends, widen in the center, and take the approximate shape of a square or rectangle. In the winter, with the average temperature as far below zero as the summer average is above it, the leads refreeze before they have time to widen and assume a more generous shape.

Walt told us also that the cracklike leads would vary in width from a few yards to perhaps several miles. They are often very long, sometimes meandering for miles across the surface of the ice. Polynyas also vary in size, from small ponds the size of a small suburban house lot to huge lakes hundreds of yards in diameter.

Walt had flown over the Arctic Ocean many times before our trip. He told us that these openings are frequent and that we ought to find one every few miles. But this did not seem to be the case. Beyond the first 60 miles or so of the pack, where the ice was loose and shifting, we had not seen a single opening that appeared large enough to be of any value.

As my operation order read: "The military usefulness of an ocean area is dependent on at least periodic access to the surface." It was this access to the surface of the Arctic that it was our primary task to develop and demonstrate on this cruise.

But as we glided along beneath endless miles of ice that Sunday morning in August, we might as well have been beneath the peaceful waters of Long Island Sound. We could cruise in this fashion for thousands of miles without difficulty, for it doesn't really matter to a submerged submarine whether she is in the Arctic or the Caribbean. But unless we could reach the surface, we could not operate. A submarine deep beneath the surface of the Arctic Ocean cannot transmit or receive on her radio. She cannot observe the weather or detect aircraft or launch missiles. In short, she cannot act as a military agent.

The background of earlier attempts was not especially encouraging. The handful of successful surfacings by Waldo Lyon's San Diego submarines in the 40s had been made near the edge of the pack, where the openings were not really polynyas but rather gaps among the loosely scattered floes. Daring as these efforts had been in light of the crude equipment available, they did not give us much to work on. For example, on the *Carp,* water had been blown out of the central ballast tank to raise the ship vertically. Our calculations and experiments had shown that this procedure, no matter how carefully undertaken, would make the *Skate* rise so fast that any accidental contact with the ice would probably be disastrous.

The first attempt to surface a nuclear submarine in a polynya **was** no more encouraging. The *Nautilus,* the fall before, had seriously damaged her periscopes colliding with a small block of ice as she made a cautious ascent and had nearly been forced to turn back as a result.

All of these things were much in our minds as we sailed northward. How soon should we attempt to surface? After we had reached the Pole? There was nothing between us and the Pole now, and an attempted surfacing might result in damage that would force us to return. And what would we have accomplished? Nothing. I concluded that it was better to reach the Pole first, then experiment.

I glanced at my watch. It was nearly time for Sunday morning services. It is my duty to see that religious services are held on board when the ship is under way on Sunday. As the one who must conduct these services, I have always found them to bring me much comfort and reward.

Although I am a Presbyterian, I have found the Episcopal *Book of Common Prayer* the best guide for a service that is to be informal and conducted by a layman. Its beautiful and simple language helps us gain a sense of reverence when we are far removed from the usual surroundings of worship. On Sunday mornings that have found us hundreds of feet below the surface of the sea and thousands of miles from home and family, we have found particular strength in the responses of the *Venite:*

> In his hand are all the corners of the earth; and the strength of the hills is his also.
>
> The sea is his, and he made it; and his hands prepared the dry land.
>
> O come, let us worship and fall down. . . .

On this Sunday morning beneath the ice, without doubt the most self-reliant of us felt some need of contact with the force we may define in different ways, but all know, at least at times, we need.

On my way to the crew's mess hall I passed the ice machine. There Walt Wittmann was watching the endless procession of ice floes and pressure ridges overhead.

"Captain," he said, "for the past few minutes we've been

showing signs of coming in to a loose area, there's been a good bit of open water. . . . There! Look at that one!"

A thin black line stretched on and on, then stopped as suddenly as it started. It had remained on the machine for nearly a minute.

"That's the biggest one we've seen," Walt said eagerly. "I don't know how many more we'll see like it."

I then thought how badly this crew needed something to shake them out of the lingering disappointment of yesterday. No submarine had ever surfaced so far north. I suddenly changed my mind.

"We'll have church later," I said. "Call away the plotting party."

For weeks we had been drilling a special group to do what would be required at this critical point in our cruise. They had not expected it so soon, but they all moved quickly to their positions.

Bill Cowhill went to the diving officer's stand. Lieutenant Al Kelln took charge of the ice machine. In over-all charge was Nick.

We moved slowly back and forth under the suspected polynya, plotting our motion as we went and attempting to draw a picture of the opening. We were new at the job, and our picture had flaws, but we got the rough shape. Finally we came to a stop beneath its center.

I raised the periscope against the pressure of the sea. There was a huge jellyfish, staring into the periscope, whose graceful floating showed us beyond the limited precision of our instruments that we had truly come to a halt.

Lowering the periscope, I took one last look at the chart. I then had Nick ask Al Kelln if all was clear overhead.

Al, with an expressionless face, held up his left hand, with index finger and thumb forming a circle and the remaining three fingers raised.

PART II

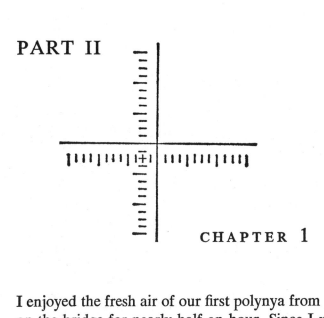

CHAPTER 1

I enjoyed the fresh air of our first polynya from my vantage point on the bridge for nearly half an hour. Since I was about 25 feet above the water, I was able to see something of the ice pack beyond our immediate vicinity. There were other polynyas in our neighborhood; some seemed even larger than the one chance had guided us to. The impression, however, was of an infinite sea of ice. Like the pieces of a gigantic jigsaw puzzle, the floes stretched on and on in all direction as far as I could see. In the distance the white of the overcast sky blended with the ice to blur the horizon.

I looked down at the lake of blue water in which we lay. It seemed an insignificant puddle in this enormous ice plain, and the *Skate* floating in the center of it looked pathetically small. Under the sea we had been in our element. There, wrapped in our man-made cocoon of steel and instruments, we had no such sense of overwhelming vastness. Here on the surface our puniness was exposed and our weakness apparent.

Still, in the open, the atmosphere of tension which had been with us since midnight seemed to lift with every breath of the fresh cool air of the arctic summer. Beneath the surface, we had felt tensely responsible for every move; up here we felt released, free.

Walt Wittmann came to the bridge, bubbling with enthusiasm. He was dressed in his fur parka, complete with raccoon-fur hood. He carried a can for ice samples, a thermometer attached to a long knotted line, and a pair of binoculars. Walt is devoted to the study of ice in the way a painter is devoted to his art. It absorbs him and delights him, both esthetically and intellectually. To be floating in a stretch of open water deep inside the ice pack, where no man had ever been before, was an experience he just couldn't take calmly.

Climbing down to the main deck, he busied himself with lowering his thermometer over the side and measuring the water temperature at varying depths. He estimated the strength and direction of the faint breeze wafting over us and carefully recorded all of his data in a small notebook. He was soon joined by Dr. LaFond, who called me to ask if he could go over to the ice to get some samples.

Skate is equipped with an inflatable rubber boat for just such taxi purposes. Collapsed and rolled up, it is about the size of a good-size duffle bag and can be stowed readily. Blown up, it is 12 feet long, 6 feet wide, and will carry seven men. It must be paddled by hand and is neither graceful nor very seaworthy, but it does its job.

In a few minutes, Wittmann, LaFond, and Paul Dornberg were on their way over to "shore." Soon after, we were joined by a pair of white sea birds that I could not identify. However, I saw Dr. LaFond examining them closely through his binoculars and making notes in his book. He later told me they were ice mews (*Larus eburneus*). It embarrassed me somewhat that while I stood idly on the bridge, reflecting on the puniness of man and his works in the midst of an overwhelming environment, our scientists were busy measuring and identifying, to gain that power over one's environment that knowledge brings.

When I went below decks, I found others of our civilian scientists busy on similar tasks. Our cheerful, chunky gravity expert Dave Scull was carefully measuring the exact pull of the earth's gravitational force upon us. In this way, Dave was able to detect even slight irregularities in the form of the earth. Working close to him was our expert on underwater sound Fran Weigle, from the Navy Laboratory at New London. Fran, a dark, quiet man in his early thirties, was engaged in checking the sound-transmission qualities of the arctic water. I felt like the grasshopper of the fable, surrounded by industrious ants.

Lunch that day was a festive affair. A surge of enthusiasm had replaced the depressed spirits of the day before. Accomplishment had taken the edge off disappointment. Our achievement imparted a new confidence—individual and collective— which could be felt all over the ship.

Even quiet, unexcitable Bill Layman, our chief engineer, was laughing and cracking jokes. He recalled the time we had all been in Pittsburgh together, going to school at Bettis Atomic Laboratory. All of the officers were living bachelor style in one rented house, taking turns with the cooking. One evening it had been Bill's turn to cook, and as he went out to shop I told him to buy a bottle of wine to go with dinner at my expense. When dinner was served, the wine was poured with great ritual, the bottle carefully wrapped in a napkin. Bill said apologetically he hoped I wouldn't mind, but that he had gotten carried away with the project and had bought the most expensive wine he could find. It was a 1947 Burgundy, from one of the very best vineyards. Everyone kept tasting it, sighing deeply, and sagely pronouncing it the best they had tasted. I was having a difficult time, not only worrying about how much this heirloom was going to cost me, but also trying to convince myself that it tasted like anything special. No expert on wines at all, I was ready to admit that I just didn't know a good wine from a cheap one. From the intent gaze of my dinner companions, I gathered that they were in on some sort of plot that I wasn't aware of. The napkin was finally whipped off to reveal a quart bottle of Chianti, plainly marked at seventy-five cents.

After lunch Nicholson shot the sun several times through the periscope, which even on the surface is easier to use than a sextant. On the chart he carefully plotted in the lines of position he obtained from his calculation of these sights. They passed very close to the heavily marked circle that indicated our position estimated by dead reckoning. Close to it a lighter circle showed our position as reckoned by the magic of the inertial navigation system. Everything seemed to be checking—dead reckoning, inertial navigation, and now celestial navigation. It was a comforting feeling. It meant that Prins Karls Forland was no longer our last touch with navigational reality. For now we had another place on the chart where we could put down our hand and say: "Here we know where we are."

I decided it was time for us to be on our way. I went to the bridge for a last look at our surroundings. The rubber boat was deflated and stowed, the hatches on deck were closed, and no one remained above decks but Bill Cowhill and me. I gazed again at the icy horizon to the north. The ice field seemed to stretch on forever. How far could I see? Perhaps 6 miles at the most. And the Pole—how far was it? Over 400 miles.

I climbed down the narrow ladder into the control center. There all was in readiness. Bill Cowhill had planned this maneuver for weeks. Normally a submarine dives with considerable speed, using her forward momentum to plane herself under. But with no room to move, *Skate* would have to reverse the procedure which had brought her to the surface, and by a delicate balancing of ballast submerge straight down.

Cowhill came down from the bridge and shut the heavy watertight hatch. The indicator light on a board to my left indicated all openings to sea were closed. Cowhill rang the diving signal, and the raucous *ah*–uu–*ga* of the klaxon echoed through the ship. Chief Dornberg, standing at the control levers, pulled those that opened the top of the ballast tanks and allowed them to flood. We could hear the roar of water as it rushed into the empty tanks.

I looked through the periscope at the bow and stern of the *Skate*. They were slowly beginning to settle into the calm blue water. I looked at the edges of the polynya. In two hours there had been no sign of change in its oval shape. Not a ripple had marred the surface of our pond; no stray floating blocks of ice had threatened us. It had been a friendly place. As we sank farther only our periscope remained to show our presence.

I saw the two sea birds circle the periscope just before the water closed silently over its top.

CHAPTER 2

When the *Skate* had sunk far enough to be clear of any deep-reaching pressure ridges I gave the order to open the steam to the turbines and put power on the propellers. Soon we were moving slowly away from our location under the polynya. Looking up with the periscope I could see the darkness close in over us once more as we moved under the heavy ice. We then headed due north and speeded up.

I was anxious to hold the services which had been postponed that morning. We were soon assembled in the crew's mess hall.

I thought of a passage in the 139th Psalm that seemed especially appropriate for this day, and I decided to read it at the close of the service:

> Whither shall I go from thy Spirit?
> or whither shall I flee from thy presence?
> If I ascend up into heaven, thou art there:
> if I make my bed in hell, behold, thou art there.
> If I take the wings of the morning, and dwell in the uttermost parts of the sea;
> Even there shall thy hand lead me, and thy right hand shall hold me. . . .

In *The Age of Faith,* Will Durant commented that man must reason in order to advance, but that he must believe in order to live. The reason of man created the *Skate,* and only cool reason can make her work. But this is not enough. We who are in charge of this creature of reason must often lean upon our faith in a Presence beyond reason to find the strength of spirit and will to fulfill our duties "in the uttermost parts of the sea."

After services, Bill Layman and I sat side by side on a small red-cushioned bench in the maneuvering room to discuss a matter that had given us much concern of late.

The nuclear power plant is basically a delicate machine. Although it is capable of producing enormous amounts of power for long periods, it is also subject to destruction by a few minutes of improper operation. Not violent destruction in the explosive sense—this, thank goodness, is literally impossible—but destruction that, although no evidence of damage might be seen, would completely disable the plant as a source of power.

To protect them against just this sort of accident, submarine nuclear power plants have been designed with a network of automatic safety devices which cause the control rods to drop into the reactor right to the bottom, shutting it down entirely whenever events occur that might make operation unsafe.

But the automatic safety devices may themselves operate improperly, and may shut down the reactor when there is no real reason to do so. Once shut down, for whatever reason, a nuclear power plant cannot be restarted like a stalled automobile. The reactor itself must again be made to produce power by carefully withdrawing the control rods; steam must be generated and the turbines reactivated. This is not a quick or easy process. With a well-trained crew and no difficulties it can take close to an hour, and with the slightest hindrance this time can be much longer.

While the reactor is shut down there is only one source of power for lighting and ventilation, for the bank of air-purifying machines that keep the air breathable, and—perhaps most important—for the motors, pumps, instruments, and heaters required to bring the main power plant to life again: a storage battery, much smaller than that on a conventional submarine.

What happens if the nuclear plant cannot be started before the battery is exhausted? In the design of the *Skate* even this circumstance is provided for. The ship also contains a diesel engine to provide auxiliary power and to generate life-giving electric power while the main plant is shut down. But diesel engines require huge quantities of air in order to run. They cannot be used submerged unless an air-gulping snorkel pipe can be extended to the surface—and of course this cannot be done while the submarine is sealed under the ice.

All of us knew that this risk was inherent in taking the submarine under the arctic ice. We had been mainly concerned with the risk of major calamities—collision, fire, steam leaks, and radiation. But so dependent were we upon the intricate mechanics of our ship that even minor malfunctioning in her safety equipment could place us in grave peril. If the plant should suddenly shut down—for whatever reason—while we were under the ice, our lives would depend upon restarting the plant before the storage battery gave out or finding an opening in which the *Skate* could be brought to the surface and her diesel engine operated. If we should fail, we would find a cold and air-less tomb as surely as had the men of the S–4, trapped in the shallow waters of Cape Cod Bay and unable to surface or renew their exhausted battery.

We hoped to cope with this emergency by carefully recording each opening we passed, so that we might retrace our path to it if we had trouble. This plan was what Bill and I were discussing.

"I was watching the trace early this morning," Bill said, "and I'm not sure our scheme is going to work too well."

"I know what you mean," I replied. "Too many long stretches with no opening big enough to do any good."

"Too many long stretches without any opening at all," Bill said.

"Probably better to go on ahead in those cases."

"Go ahead—and hope," Bill said, and that about summed it up.

As I walked forward through the engine room I looked at the pieces of machinery on which we were betting our lives. I stopped by a sleek gray turbine, humming efficiently behind its shining dials and burnished fittings, pouring out the electric power that enabled the *Skate* to live. In the harmony of every part with its function, it was a thing of beauty.

I thought of the men—most of whom I knew—who had spent years of their lives designing this ship and this machinery. I thought of the gray-haired admiral whose relentless will had made it possible, and of the sign behind his desk:

Our doubts are traitors
And make us lose the good we oft might win. . . .

The thin blue folder that contained our operation order lay on the green felt of the wardroom table. Gathered with me for an informal meeting were all the officers who were not on watch.

"Let me read this again so we'll all know what we're authorized to do," I said.

If the Pole is reached by the fourteenth of August you are authorized to proceed to the vicinity of Drifting Ice Station Alfa, attempt to communicate with its personnel, and further to attempt to surface near enough so that contact can be made.

The United States was at that time maintaining two survey stations on the polar ice pack in connection with the International Geophysical Year. Such stations are simply camps established on the surface of the ice for scientific observation. As they are carried along by the drift of the ice pack, at the rate of 2 or 3 miles a day, the men at the stations are able to gather much data, including soundings, in otherwise inaccessible parts of the Arctic Ocean.

Such camps did not originate with the International Geophysical Year. Four decades earlier, Vilhjalmur Stefansson and his sturdy assistant Storker Storkerson conceived the idea of camping on an arctic ice floe in order to take scientific data as they drifted through the polar sea. Although Stefansson was prevented from participating by an attack of typhoid, in 1918, Storkerson sledged 200 miles north from the Alaska coast where he established a camp in which he and his four men lived for nearly six months while drifting some 400 miles. In 1937 the Russians established one of the early stations only 34 miles from the North Pole. This station drifted for almost a year, finally freeing itself from the pack and coming to rest on the east coast of Greenland over 1100 nautical miles from where it had started.

After World War II another Soviet ice station discovered one of the most spectacular underwater features of the Arctic. Drifting slowly over the 2-mile-deep central basin, the Russians noted a sudden shoaling in their soundings. They passed over a huge ridge before their soundings began to deepen again. Later soundings confirmed the presence of a gigantic underwater mountain range crossing the basin from Greenland to the New Siberian Islands. The Soviets named the mountain range the Lomonosov, after the eighteenth-century Russian scientist.

The two US stations, *Alfa* (that's the official spelling, however classical scholars may wince) and *Bravo,* were manned jointly by Air Force and civilian personnel. Of the two, Alfa was much closer to the North Pole. At that time it was about 300 miles from the Pole in the direction of Alaska. The idea of finding one of these stations—a pinpoint in five-and-a-half million square miles of frozen waste—from underneath the ice had seemed so fantastic to me that I had never before seriously discussed it with my officers. However, Commander Bob McWethy, who had written our operation order, had included it, "in case we were feeling really ambitious."

"There's nothing in this operation order that's mandatory," I said. "Everything is left to our judgment. How about it, do you think we ought to take a chance on Alfa?"

I knew there was no need to ask. There was a unanimously affirmative shout in reply. Nicholson, who as navigator would have the hardest job—to find the station—hesitated a moment and said: "I've given this a good bit of thought, and I think we can find it. After we go to the Pole, we should try to surface somewhere near Alfa and talk to them on radio."

Al Kelln, our electronics officer, said: "That shouldn't be any trouble. I've got their radio frequency and call letters, and we should be close enough to get through loud and clear."

Bill Layman asked, "How good is our information on where Alfa is now?"

"I have their predicted positions during the next few days," I said. "But I don't know how accurate the predictions'll be."

"Only need to be out a few miles to make it impossible to find them," said Kelln.

"That's where my idea comes in," said Nick. He explained that if we surfaced within a few miles of Alfa we could take radio direction-finder bearings on her radio signals. "Then we can submerge and just run down the bearing line until we find it!"

"How will we know when we're there?" asked Dave Boyd dubiously.

"Well, I'm not sure about that yet," Nick admitted. "We may have to have a little luck."

CHAPTER 3

The next morning was Monday, August 11. With continued good fortune we should reach the North Pole by evening. Breakfast found a cheery group of six talking with animation over orange juice, hot cakes, and sausage. And coffee, of course. The Navy lives on coffee.

Dr. LaFond was talking about the device he carried in the *Skate*'s superstructure for measuring the clarity of the water. "It's amazing," he said, "the water up here is as clear as any ocean water I've ever measured."

"How's that gadget of yours work, Doc?" asked Pat Garner, a new officer who had reported on board shortly before we left New London.

"Just a long metal tube with a light at one end and a light meter at the other. The amount of light that gets through is an indication of the clarity of the water."

"What difference does it make?" asked Pat with his usual good-natured smile.

"It's one of the ways to tell about the water movements up here," answered LaFond. "We don't know too much about how the water comes in and goes out."

While this conversation went on at the far end of the table Nick told me he was off for more sleep. "Before I turn in I want to tell you about the carbon monoxide reading. It's up a bit—about sixty parts per million. Nobody is sure whether there is really something wrong or it's only the gauge."

When the *Skate* is submerged for more than a few hours we must keep the air breathable by artificial means. Oxygen is renewed by bleeding it slowly into the ship from pressurized bottles. Carbon dioxide, the waste product of breathing, is removed by a scrubbing machine which absorbs it from the atmosphere and pumps it over the side, where it dissolves into the sea. Carbon monoxide, formed mainly by the incomplete combustion of cigarette smoking, is burned to carbon dioxide by passing it through a special heating device, and this carbon dioxide is then removed by the regular scrubber.

Of course we could largely eliminate the carbon monoxide problem by simply not allowing people to smoke. But in ships that are intended to remain submerged and sealed from the atmosphere for a month at a time the total elimination of smoking is neither practical nor desirable. The equipment is designed to allow everyone on board to smoke as much as he wants at any time.

This battery of air-purification equipment is monitored by a large group of instruments designed to indicate the concentration of the various impurities in the air as well as the oxygen content.

Carbon monoxide is an insidious poison. It has no taste, color, or smell, yet if it comprises as little as one tenth of 1 per cent of the atmosphere, it will be fatal to any living creature within a few minutes. Great care must be taken to keep it to a minimum. This morning the indication showed it several parts per million over the allowed amount, and we were checking to see whether the measuring instrument was wrong or whether something had gone wrong in the burning equipment.

I went down the stairway leading to the crew's quarters and into a small room which contained the air-purification equipment. There I found Engineman Jim Brissette checking the operation of the burner. Brissette is a short, ruggedly built man, who, by this stage of the cruise, had grown a splendid Ulysses Grant beard. He is also one of those men who can fix almost anything mechanical without half trying.

Brissette was checking the inlet and outlet temperatures, the operation of the dampers, and the air flow through the carbon monoxide burner. He stood up and wiped his hands on a cloth. "Can't see anything wrong with it, Captain," he said.

The small machinery-filled room was spotlessly clean, brightly lighted, and looked like a small research laboratory. Brissette was in charge here and the condition of the room reflected his skill and energy. "Then I'm sure there's nothing wrong with it," I said with a smile, and left completely relieved of concern.

Any modern ship is dependent on a highly trained and competent crew, but here in the *Skate,* traveling beneath a continent of ice, we carried interdependence to its ultimate. All of the men sealed in this bubble of steel are completely dependent on Jim Brissette's air-purification machinery. Over one hundred men are staking their lives on the fact that Brissette knows what he is doing. He in turn is dependent upon the others. They have faith in each other, faith in their competence as a team.

What sort of men are these? What sort of training have they had? Well, some are career Navy men, often veterans of conventional submarines who have since had up to two years of training in nuclear power. Many of our crew had served on the *Nautilus* before the *Skate* was built. The younger nuclear-power men have had a shorter, more standardized training, consisting of six months at the Navy's nuclear-power school in New London, followed by six more months at one of the AEC prototype power plants, in Idaho or West Milton, New York.

The average age of the entire crew is twenty-eight and about two thirds of them are married. All but a few are high school graduates, although only a few have had any college—none more than two years. Roughly a quarter of them own their own homes around New London.

These men have been chosen especially for nuclear submarines, and they are justly proud of it. They have been chosen from the submarine service—itself an all-volunteer force with proud traditions and high standards. Collectively, I have never known a better or more spirited crew.

As the afternoon and evening drew on, the tension and excitement in the crew built up. Navigator Nicholson announced on the loudspeaker system that if all went well, we should be at the Pole shortly after midnight.

Everyone was up and about as the *Skate* drove northward at better than 16 knots. The depth gauge read 260 feet as we skimmed along under heavy ice with almost no openings. No matter now—the goal of a year's work and planning lay just a few miles away.

The crew down in the inertial navigation room studied the flickering green signals of their cathode tubes as the delicate sensing instruments of the system showed us approaching ever closer to that part of the globe where every direction is south. Carefully, they counted the tiny green dots winking by and plotted the resulting numbers. Slowly they translated these results to navigational terms.

"Only a mile to go now, Captain," Zane Sandusky commented as I approached his machine.

"This course look good?" I asked.

"You're right on the nose—you'll split it right in two," Zane said exuberantly.

I walked up to the control center and announced our distance to the Pole on the speaker system. I turned to Al Kelln, the officer of the deck. "Let's slow to five knots, Al—we want to hit this one right on the money."

The ring of the engine annunciators sounded loud in the quiet room. Nick called forward from the chart desk: "One minute to go."

Our clocks were set on Greenwich Civil Time, four hours later than the time in New London.

Nicholson gave me the signal and I counted down over the loudspeakers: ". . . Four, three, two, MARK. At one forty-seven Greenwich time on 12 August 1958 the *Skate* has reached the northernmost part of our planet. My congratulations to each one of you, but this is only the beginning. Before we are through we are going to demonstrate that a submarine can come into this ice pack, operate at will, surface when it wants to, and carry out whatever mission our country requires."

We immediately put the rudder over and swung slowly left to reach the course for Drift Station Alfa.

CHAPTER 4

Seldom had the ice seemed so heavy and so thick as it did in the immediate area of the Pole. For days we had searched in vain for a suitable opening to surface in. The log Walt Wittmann kept to describe ice conditions tells the dreary story:

" . . . probably the roughest ice yet encountered . . . no openings of any size."

" . . . ice very closely compacted with heavy pressure ridges on every hand. . . ."

" . . . first opening of any kind for some time but much too small to use. . . ."

This continued through the morning of Tuesday the twelfth. We crept along at 5 knots, investigating every possibility, however remote. At eight-thirty in the morning, Pat Garner called me aft to the ice machine where he was on watch. Garner said: "I don't know whether you want to fool with this one or not," he told me, "but I wanted you to see it."

A short black line had appeared on the tape, so short that previously we would not have considered it. But now circumstances were different.

I decided to have a closer look. The plotting party was called away and we were soon doubling back under the opening, carefully plotting out its shape. It was small, no doubt about it.

Finally we halted under the center of the opening and the periscope was raised. I could barely suppress a gasp of shock. On either side of us hung down huge blocks of ice, jagged blocks turned on edge, rafted chunks 10 feet thick piled one on top of the other—and all looking just a few yards away.

Perhaps the instruments were right and my judgment through the periscope wrong, but I simply could not bring myself to try to maneuver the *Skate* up through these monstrous frozen jaws.

"Flood her down, we're moving on," I said.

It was easy to read the disappointment in everyone's face, but I could see no alternative.

Twice more that Tuesday morning we went through the same ordeal. The tedious weaving, the cautious halt, the tense ascent, observation with the periscope, the decision to go on.

I had to remember that we were nearly 5000 miles from home, and that our sole hope of seeing it again lay in preserving the fragile metal capsule in which we were encased. So long as we remained deep we were comparatively safe, but when we tried to brave the heavy ice and thread our way to the surface, we put the safety of our ship in peril. Was it worth the danger simply to prove it could be done?

The day wore on into afternoon. We were now more than 30 miles from the Pole.

Shortly after lunch we found another small stretch of water. Again the periscope presented the same terrifying vista. But this time I hesitated. Perhaps the broad polynya in which we had surfaced on Sunday was the kind you see 500 miles from the Pole. Perhaps the kind I was seeing today was the only kind we would ever find this far north. If so, we should find out once and for all if it was possible to use one.

"Start her up slowly, Bill," I said. Immediately the control center quieted and an atmosphere of tension gripped the room.

For a moment I had misgivings. Perhaps I had acted on impulse. But I was resolved to go up.

This time I could not afford the safety of lowering the periscope as we approached the ice—I desperately needed it to see what we were doing. Here I needed no hovering jellyfish for reference. The ice blocks served the purpose all too well.

Slowly, agonizingly slowly, we came up. Bill Cowhill's voice sounded its monotonous dirge of the decreasing depths. On every side the ice seemed to be closing in about us as we ascended through this frozen canyon. Yet Nick told me calmly that although the hole was small, our position looked good, and assured me we had open water above.

Hopefully I tilted the prism of the periscope upward. There was only heavy gloom to be seen. The ice on our port side was so heavy it was dead black, with none of the usual blue or green translucence. It resembled an enormous velvet curtain hanging down in dark folds. My heart was hammering and my mouth was dry.

I looked at Nicholson and Cowhill. Both were perfectly calm outwardly. Did they feel the same apprehension?

Finally I could see the surface of the water lapping at the edges of the ice. Now I had to lower the periscope to protect it from damage.

"How close *is* that ice to port?" I asked, as the scope went down.

"Pretty close now, Captain," said Louis Kleinlein, who had been estimating the distance by sonar. "But I can't really tell any more."

Bill Cowhill said quietly that we were hanging at 45 feet. I raised the periscope quickly and focused it on the menacing cliff of ice to port. There it was—less than 10 yards away! There was nothing to do. We were slowly drifting down upon it. There was no time to escape. For the first time, we were going to hit.

I thought immediately of the propellers and rudder. Here the ship was most vulnerable; just a touch could damage them irreparably. Quickly I turned the periscope aft. Everyone could hear my sigh of relief. By the greatest good fortune, the wall of ice we were being set against curved slightly away from the stern of the *Skate*—as though it had been designed to accommodate her without injury.

With a gentle thud the side of the ship struck the wall of ice. No harm was done. We hung with just the periscope and the top of the sail out of the water.

We were at the edge of a small, irregularly shaped polynya.

It appeared doubtful that it was large enough to hold the *Skate* safely when completely surfaced.

Now the reason for this strange canyonlike ice formation became immediately apparent. The right- and left-hand sides of the polynya were hummocked with heavy pressure ridges. Without doubt colossal pressure had been exerted at this point, grinding two large floes together, and forming ridges both above and below the surface. (The general rule is that the below-water ridge will be four to five times as deep as the above-water ridge is high.) Then the pressure had been released, allowing the two floes to drift apart. It was between the two rafted and jumbled edges that we had come to the surface.

As I looked again toward the stern, I noted that it was beginning to pivot toward the ice. There was nothing to do. To have applied power to the propellers could have been disastrous. Then, even as I winced in anticipation of the impact, the stern swung *under* the edge of the ice, and came to rest once more without the rudder or propellers being touched.

Still, this was dangerous. Even though momentarily safe in this indentation in the floe, the propellers were painfully close to the ice. Apparently there was only one safe course—to flood down and get out. But I was like a mountain-climber with a tenuous foothold at the top of a treacherous peak. To hold on was dangerous; to give up meant we might never reach it again. This was the top of the world, where no submarine had ever been before. If we gave up, no one might try it again for years. I wanted desperately to hang on.

After swinging under the ice astern, the *Skate* seemed to reach an equilibrium. But how could we complete our surfacing? We were like a whale awash, with just the hump of our sail out of the water. Surfacing would require extricating the stern from the ice. The topside rudder, jutting up above the deckline, was especially vulnerable if caught under the ice. The thought of a damaged and jammed rudder under the ice pack was enough to send chills up my back. What if the rudder were jammed at, say, full right? We might wander in circles for many a week, but we'd never come close to getting out of the ice pack. And there would be nothing we could do to repair it under the sea.

The alternatives soon became clear: I must either flood down and leave this treacherous place, put power on the propellers in an attempt to work the stern away from the ice shelf, or remain where I was, partially surfaced.

I decided on the last choice. In this position we could use our radio, take sights with our periscope sextant, and put up our ventilation piping. In other words, we could accomplish most of the things we wanted to do.

There were, however, problems. A submarine floating at 45 feet is in a delicate state of equilibrium. A few hundred pounds of change in weight can send her on her way up or down. Up meant damage to the precious rudder; down meant the loss of our foothold.

Bill Cowhill adjusted the trim of the ship carefully. The current continued to press us in against the wall of ice on our port side. Although precariously perched, we seemed safe enough for the moment.

Nicholson took over the periscope. A low whistle was his only comment before he started snapping hasty sun elevations through the intermittent clouds. After taking several shots he turned the periscope over to me and went aft to his chart table. I then attempted to estimate the weather more accurately for quartermaster John Medaglia, so that he could log it. Fortunately we had wired a thermometer to a radio antenna so that we could read it through the periscope. It was 33 degrees above zero. The wind was light, judging from the ripples—perhaps two or three knots. The ice was in motion, which gave the illusion of a current to port. But the force that moved the ice must have come from another area; there was not enough wind here to move anything. It occurred to me that in this situation the polynya we were in might close with little or no warning.

I immediately drafted a message to be sent to the Navy Department. They had not heard from us since we entered the pack:

REACHED NORTH GEOGRAPHIC POLE AUGUST ELEVENTH X
NOW IN POLYNYA ABOUT FORTY MILES FROM POLE X ALL
WELL

Chief Radioman Dale McCord sat down in the radio room
and tapped out the signals for:

ANY SHIP OR ANY STATION X THIS IS THE USS SKATE X WE
HAVE A MESSAGE TO SEND

Almost immediately came this reply:

THIS IS RADIO MANILA X HEAR YOU LOUD AND CLEAR X RE-
QUEST YOU REPEAT YOUR NAME

It was the US Navy operator in the Philippines. He couldn't
understand what the *Skate,* supposedly stationed in the Atlantic,
was doing in his ocean! We repeated our call. He answered:

UNDERSTAND SUBMARINE SKATE X SEND YOUR MESSAGE

Apparently with the news of the *Nautilus* in the air the operator at Manila was willing to believe anything coming from a
nuclear submarine.

I came into the wardroom to sit down. Only then did I realize
how tired I was. The thought of more effort to come exhausted
me.

LaFond and Wittmann were talking excitedly about this new
polynya with the enthusiasm of small boys at the circus. When I
walked into the room, they both extended their hands in congratulation. It was deeply gratifying to know that these men,
so recently members of our group, understood the difficulty and
significance of what we had just done.

In a moment Nick joined us with a message he had drafted to
Station Alfa:

REQUEST YOUR EXACT POSITION X ALSO REQUEST INFORMA-
TION ON NUMBER AND SIZE OF POLYNYAS YOUR VICINITY

"That ought to do it, Nick," I said, scribbling my signature on the message.

I felt deeply tired, and Nick looked tired. He had gotten less than four hours sleep in the last seventy-two. I had done better than that, but not much. The cup of hot tea I was drinking seemed to make me even sleepier.

"Nick, this is where you and I both get some sleep," I said. "I'd like to stay here until we get an answer from Alfa, anyway."

After leaving instructions for the officers of the deck to watch our buoyancy carefully and to be alert for any sign of ice movement, I went to my room. The knowledge that we were at the surface, however precariously, eased my mind. I felt more relaxed than I had in three days, and slept for fourteen hours.

During all of that time the regular sea watches continued, the reactor and turbines were kept running, the galley continued its steady service, a torpedo was pulled from its tube and opened for servicing. In fact, all of the normal, busy routine of the ship kept up just as though we had been traveling under the sea.

But the *Skate* herself hung motionless, perched just below the surface of the water between two cliffs of ice, her periscopes, antennas, and ventilation pipes piercing the still surface like the pales of a picket fence at the edge of our small lake.

While I was asleep the answer from Station Alfa was received.

NO OBSERVATIONS FOR SEVERAL DAYS SO POSITION NOT KNOWN X BEST ESTIMATE NEAR EIGHTY FIVE NORTH ONE THREE SIX WEST X MANY POLYNYAS IN VICINITY BUT BEST ONLY FIFTY YARDS FROM OUR MAIN BUILDINGS

Dave Boyd was sitting in the wardroom and I handed the message to him. He chuckled and said: "How do you go about finding a place that doesn't know where it is?"

"Wonder why they haven't been able to take any observations," I said. "I guess the overcast must really be heavy over there."

"I suppose so," said Dave, "but at least it's good news about the polynya. Wouldn't that be something if we could find the one only fifty yards away? It'd be like surfacing right in their camp!"

At 9:30 A.M. on Wednesday, August 13, we finally made preparations to leave our hard-gained position at the top of the world. It was the morning of our fourth day in the ice pack; although it was not yet beginning to feel precisely like home, our awe was slowly diminishing.

Flooding down was relatively simple. Down we drifted, much faster than we had dared come up. I looked at the walls of ice as we dropped away and wondered if I would have the nervous stamina to get into such a tight place again. Soon the aquamarine and black of the ice walls gave way to the deep azure of the arctic water. We were free of the ice, and turned once more in the direction of Alfa.

Until we reached the Pole, our fathometer had traced the distant floor of the North Eurasian Basin, which averages close to 12,000 feet in depth. To gain an idea how the *Skate* looked in this ocean, imagine a kitchen matchstick suspended about two inches below the ceiling of a 10-foot-high room. The ceiling would be the ice, the floor the bottom of the sea, and the humble matchstick our submarine. It is a vision which makes man and his works seem pretty minute.

Almost as soon as we left the Pole, however, our fathometer began to record the gentle rise of the foothills of the Lomonosov Ridge. We were coming out of the Eurasian Basin. By the time we had gained our foothold at the surface on Tuesday afternoon the soundings had reached a shelf at 7000 feet.

Now, as we resumed our journey toward Alfa, we could watch the profile of the mountain chain taking shape on the traveling tape of our fathometer. The tape, about 2 feet high, made a fine drawing board for the stylus as it sketched a rising series of jagged peaks and gullies.

I could envision the lofty range below us as we floated slowly over it. It was both beautiful and awe-inspiring—even frightening—in the way it dwarfed into insignificance the tiny steel egg cruising above its towering peaks.

What a magnificent sight this Lomonosov would be if set out on dry land! More than 1000 miles in length, it soars in places to heights more than 10,000 feet above its surrounding plain. In its size and the sharpness of its slopes and peaks it could be compared with the dramatic Andes chain of South America. But hidden under the frozen wastes of the Arctic it has little chance to display its beauty; only through the vicarious sight of instruments will man ever feel its presence and know its form.

CHAPTER 5

By breakfast time on Thursday we were within 30 miles of Alfa—unless both our navigation and Alfa's estimate of its own location were drastically in error. We slowed and began to look about for a place to surface. This time we were in a noticeably looser area than we had been at the Pole; by eight-thirty we were maneuvering under a promising opening.

Our location was roughly halfway between the North Pole and Alaska; we had penetrated to the other side of the world. We were also in part of the Arctic that explorer Vilhjalmur Stefansson had named the Zone of Comparative Inaccessibility because it was the region most remote from approach by ship —more remote than the North Pole itself. So far as I knew, not even a drifting ship, locked in the ice, had ever reached the Zone of Inaccessibility.

As we floated cautiously underneath the opening in the ice I raised the periscope to examine the ice above. Here was no canyon of ice, but a polynya like that we had found our first day in the ice pack. The edge of the lake was visible and looked no thicker than the average floe.

In a few minutes the periscope reached the open air. I told Bill Cowhill to blow the tanks, and the *Skate* rose quickly to the surface. As I climbed to the bridge the open air struck my face like a damp cloth. I looked about at the ice fields stretching to the horizon in every direction. The *Skate* had reached the Zone of Inaccessibility.

In August the icefields are dotted with thousands of puddles of melt water. These evidences of the wan arctic sun range in size from a few feet in diameter to sizable ponds, and in depth from a few inches to three or four feet. (In the summer of 1894 Nansen's men found one near the *Fram* that was large enough to sail the ship's cutter in; it gave them a good bit of sport.) The water in them is surprisingly fresh; it is safe to drink. The color of the water is an aquamarine of gemlike purity.

As I stood on the bridge that morning these blue jewels were scattered in every direction over the ermine white of the floes. Two or three other polynas were also visible, looking almost black beside the cheerful azure of the ponds.

The temperature was 31 degrees, and the wind about 5 knots. The sun was obscured by a heavy low overcast, but the blue-accented white of the icefields made the bleak landscape seem almost cheerful. I passed the word for the deck hatches to be opened so that everyone could come out on deck.

As the crew began to appear from the hatches, their high spirits became immediately apparent. They gazed in wonder at the sparkling blue lake in which we rested and the pressure and worry of operating the *Skate* under the ice rolled from their backs almost visibly. Quartermaster John Medaglia, a short, dark young man with a sort of elfin charm and an infectious sense of humor, is not one to hide his wit under a bushel. He called up to the bridge: "Looks like just the place for swimming call, Captain!"

"We've just had it—you're first!" I shouted back. Four men grabbed John without delay, two taking his feet and two his arms, and started to swing him toward the icy water. Medaglia screamed protest. Fortunately for him, reason eventually prevailed, and Medaglia, in no wise chastened, was put back laughing on his feet.

There is nothing like success to heal the wounds of disappointment. I was reminded of the words of Peary in *The North Pole,* describing how he and his companions returned from their goal, back over the hundreds of miles of rafted and twisted ice floes: "We returned from the Pole to Cape Columbia in only sixteen days . . . the exhilaration of success lent wings to our sorely battered feet."

My own steps were light as I strolled to the wardroom.

There I found Nicholson working over a huge chart spread across the table. Walt Wittmann and Dave Boyd were looking over his shoulder. The position of the *Skate* was marked on the chart, and a light pencil line extended for about 10 inches from it.

"Got the bearing on Alfa with no trouble," Nick said. "There it is." He pointed to the pencil line. "By the way, his call letters are I–C–E. Pretty good, eh?"

"Yes," I said with a smile, "but how far away on that line?"

"Maybe when we leave here we could go about twenty miles on a course at right angles to this bearing," said Dave Boyd. "Then get another radio bearing and cross them. That would do it, wouldn't it?"

"Sure would," I agreed. "I only wish it wouldn't take so long. Even then it might not be absolutely precise. There could be five polynyas inside a square mile—and only one right one."

With no conclusion, we folded the chart and put it away as Jones began to set the table for lunch. As we sat eating, a messenger came in with a dispatch just received from Alfa:

WILL RUN OUTBOARD MOTORBOAT CONTINUOUSLY IN POLYNYA NEAREST CAMP

There was our answer—if only we could hear the motorboat far enough away.

"Ask Kleinlein to step in here for a moment," I told the messenger.

In a few minutes I was asking our senior sonarman, Louis Kleinlein, how far he thought he could hear an outboard motor underneath the ice. A slow smile of understanding spread over Kleinlein's cheerful face as he saw what I was driving at.

"Well, we wouldn't hear it at all unless we were submerged," he said, "but submerged we might be able to hear it five miles or so off."

After lunch I went to the bridge for some fresh air. Dr. LaFond, Walt Wittmann, and several of the crew members were over on the ice floes stretching their legs and looking over their surroundings. Wittmann and LaFond were, of course, getting their customary samples of ice and water.

Before long, Wittmann and LaFond were back, late for lunch, but as usual bubbling with enthusiasm.

"No sign of any birds today," said LaFond. "Apparently the Zone of Inaccessibility applies to them too."

I asked the men who had rowed Wittmann and LaFond back in the rubber boat to give me a lift to the ice. When they dropped me off I struck out across the floes for a bit of exercise and solitude.

I made my way to a small pressure ridge, or hummock. As I crossed it, the sight of the ship was momentarily shut out. The dominant impression was one of stillness. The *Skate* is filled with a hundred small motors, blowers, fans, generators, and other machines which combine to make a background of noise so constant that we cease to realize it is there. It is like the ticking of an alarm clock in the bedroom. But I was away from it, and away from every other noise. The breeze had dropped to almost nothing. There was simply no sound.

There was no sign of life either. No color but the white of the snow, the aquamarine of the melt ponds, and the green of an occasional block of pack ice thrust on edge by pressure and exposed like a rock in a New England meadow.

In the melt ponds the water was as transparent as the air, and the graceful folds of blue ice at the bottom could be seen plainly. Ordinarily the ice is covered with rough crystalline snow, but where melt had occurred the lovely aquamarine blue of the ice was revealed. I thought of what lay under this tranquil surface. A foot of water, perhaps 9 feet of ice, and then thousands and thousands of feet of black, icy sea water, reaching down to a bottom so remote that man would probably never know its real nature. The film of ice floating over that void was so thin in comparison that it was like the dust on the surface of the water in a rain barrel.

I walked still farther from the ship, toward a low hummock where ice was thrown up and tumbled in a hundred different postures. Some looked like the prows of ships, some like the ziggurats of ancient Babylon, some like the Druid stones of Britain. I climbed to the top of the hummock and could see in the distance the black sail of the *Skate* silhouetted against the surrounding white, lonely and incongruous.

The walking conditions were appalling. The rough snow was like mush underfoot. Even the slight exertion of my walk left me damp with perspiration, and when I stopped to look or to rest, the cold of the air penetrated my clothes and chilled me to the bone. How could De Long and his men from the *Jeannette* have crossed this ice, that summer of 1881, dragging their three boats with them? What misery it must have been, slogging their way through this slushy swampland! Every hummock a crisis, every melt pond a detour; never dry, always hungry.

And what chance would my men from the *Skate* have if we found it necessary to trek across the ice? Not even half the chance that De Long's men had. For at least they had had dogs and furs and sledges and provisions intended for overland travel. We had none of these, and little knowledge of the rudiments of arctic survival. We had put all our trust in the slim black hull that floated a few hundred yards away. Without it we would die like fish in a desert.

I recalled a memorable phrase written by William Bolitho about Christopher Columbus. The glory of Columbus, he said, was that of all adventurers, "... *to have been the tremendous outsider.*"

That was the phrase that expressed it. We were outsiders, able to exist here only for a few hours without our machines and instruments—almost as much out of our element as the first men who step out of their space ship onto the surface of the moon.

Suddenly I felt very lonely. I walked hurriedly back to the shore of our polynya and called to the officer of the deck to send the boat. Soon I was back on board. Climbing down the long steel tube into the interior of the ship I entered another world. Warmth, light, noise, and companionship were everywhere. This was home.

Everything seemed in readiness for the attempt to locate Station Alfa. Nicholson had laid out his charts with circles and lines designed to minimize our chances of missing our goal. The plotting party was stationed and ready.

The air hissed out of the ballast tanks as we started to submerge; looking forward and aft through the periscope I could see clouds of vapor where warm air coming from the tanks struck the cool atmosphere. Slowly the still water lapped higher and higher on the black hull until it disappeared. The outsider was gone.

The steam puffed into the turbines and the *Skate* moved gently ahead. As the ship settled comfortably into her element, and the air bubbles cleared from the superstructure, our underwater listening apparatus became more efficient. In a few minutes, a slow grin broke out over Kleinlein's face. He handed his ear-phones over to me. The soft *putputputput* of an outboard motor was unmistakable.

As we steered down the bearing line for Alfa, Nicholson kept a careful dead reckoning plot of the distance we had traveled. Kleinlein called out the direction of the outboard motor's noise from time to time; it seemed to remain directly ahead of us. Al Kelln kept a sharp watch on the ice machine for open water.

We were in an area where the ice pack was apparently under little or no compression. There were many polynyas that looked large enough to use. It was as though the sea, having given us nothing but trouble in finding an open spot near the Pole, was now relenting from its severity.

It was not just any polynya we wanted now, however. We were shooting for one out of thousands. The sound of the outboard grew steadily louder, but it was much harder for Kleinlein to give us an accurate bearing. His readings swung from right to left and Nick began to look concerned as he plotted them.

Then without warning the sound disappeared. Although we searched carefully in all directions it was not to be heard. Only one thing could have happened—we had passed the Drift Station, and the bulk of the *Skate*'s hull blocked off the sound astern. Ponderously the *Skate* swung her 3000 tons around and headed slowly back. Once more the *putputputput* came into the earphones.

Now we had to go more slowly and see where the noise cut off. Al Kelln watched intently to see if a polynya showed up simultaneously.

The first time there was no success. The noise cut off, but the ice machine showed nothing but solid ice overhead. We turned slowly (at this speed it took us two or three minutes just to reverse course) and make another pass. Now Kleinlein reported that the noise was all around—we couldn't be far away.

"Open water overhead!" shouted Kelln. But his joy turned to dismay as he saw that the opening was only 70 yards wide—not long enough to hold us. This couldn't be it. They said it was a big one.

Nevertheless we marked its position on the plotting sheet and turned back to pass under it again, in a different direction. As we approached we got the same encouraging sign of open water. And this time it stretched on and on and on. It was a long narrow polynya—perfectly satisfactory if we got the *Skate* positioned properly.

Up we came, no ice in sight except the ordinary floes at the edges of the sausage-shaped polynya. The hull of the *Skate* had to match this shape exactly or we would not fit.

"Port ahead one-third, starboard back one-third, right full rudder," I said, and the *Skate* obediently swung slowly to the right to align herself with the open water above.

"All stop, rudder amidships." We were just right. I could see ripples on the water above the periscope. The ice was the same distance away on either side; I could see none forward or astern.

Slowly the periscope came out of the water. We were surrounded by arctic civilization. Small brown huts dotted the ice.

A high radio antenna rose over them. The squat silo shape of a radar dome lay farther astern. Near it stood a tall pole with the American flag.

Our polynya, as we had thought, was long and thin but of good size.

And around the edge of it, as though on a racetrack, cruised a small outboard motorboat. Its occupant was waving his hat wildly.

CHAPTER 6

Hardly had the *Skate* reached the surface when the small boat was briskly maneuvered alongside, tied up, and its passenger welcomed on board. He was Major Joseph Bilotta of the Air Force, the senior military man at Alfa. Due to a misunderstanding about the time of our departure from the polynya where we had gotten our radio bearings, the Major had been in his outboard motorboat making noise for many hours. Obviously, he could have been spelled by someone else, but he didn't want to leave the lake for even a moment for fear he might miss us.

"I've never seen an eerier sight in my life," he exclaimed as he climbed on board, "than your periscope coming up in this empty lake! It was weird!"

Bilotta's craft was a white fiberglass speedboat about 12 feet long—exactly the sort that boys use to roar around lakes in summertime America. It constituted the entire Alfa navy. There was no need for anything else; although the station was located near the center of a great ocean, it was situated on a 10-foot-thick ice floe several acres in size. The only appearance made by the deep ocean over which it floated was in the form of occasional polynyas which appeared during the summer.

In the first and third polynyas we had visited, the *Skate* remained more or less in the center of the available open water by occasional gentle maneuvers with her propellers. Here at Alfa, with the prospect of a longer stay, we decided to attempt mooring to the ice. Chief Dornberg and two seamen clattered out on deck carrying half a dozen long steel stakes and a sledgehammer apiece. With Bilotta's blessing they started up the outboard and putted off to drive these mooring bars into the ice.

Bilotta was cold and tired, and Nick hustled him down to the warmth of the wardroom for coffee and cake. In the meantime we carefully parked the *Skate* alongside the ice. Lines were thrown over and made fast to the iron stakes, and the *Skate* was moored securely to the ice, 50 yards from the main camp—and less than a hundred miles from the center of Stefansson's Zone of Inaccessibility.

Down below in the wardroom I found Bilotta, a short, rugged man of about forty with an enviable thatch of brown hair, wearing a plain, olive-drab fatigue suit and no sign of rank except a gold major's maple leaf pinned to his arctic-style wool hat. He was deep in conversation with Nick, telling him the history of Alfa.

The drifting station had been established in April 1957, not long before the Geophysical Year began. The floe had then been only about 550 miles north of Barrow, Alaska. It was chosen for settlement by two famous arctic authorities: Father Thomas Cunningham, a Jesuit priest in Barrow, and Colonel Joe Fletcher of the Air Force. Fletcher and Father Cunningham had flown over the ice pack, searching until they found what looked like a sturdy floe so located that the drift of the ice would carry it through regions of interest. In the manner of Brigham Young, they pointed down and said: "This is the place." A landing was made on the floe by a ski plane. A landing strip was cleared off by an ice-scraper and its limits marked by small imported pine boughs and slowly a camp was built, all with material flown in from Alaska.

By August 1958 the station had drifted in a slow clockwise circle to a point about 900 miles northeast of Barrow. For a time there had been hope that it would reach the Pole, but the North Canadian Basin drift was already pushing it toward Canada; it was apparent that Alfa would come no closer than 300 miles from the magic point.

There were now twenty-nine men at the station; this group had been there since the early spring of '58. Half civilian and half military, the group was made up entirely of volunteers. There were no women, no families here. The scientific garrison would remain at this primitive frontier outpost for six months. Bilotta explained to us that no airplane landings could be made in the summertime, and thus no one could be evacuated under any circumstances until the autumn freeze.

By this time the wardroom clock said seven in the evening. I suddenly realized I was bone-weary. It had been a full day, to say the least. "Well, Major," I said apologetically, "I know my people would like to visit your station, and I'd like as many of yours as possible to visit the *Skate*. But right now, I'm ready for a night's sleep. Let's make out a rough schedule for tomorrow and call it a day," I said.

The Major looked at his wristwatch and frowned. "The night's pretty well shot, Commander," he said. "It's nine o'clock in the morning!"

In a moment both of us realized what was wrong. The *Skate* was keeping Greenwich Civil (English) time while Alfa was keeping Alaskan time, which was ten hours earlier. So, while it was nine in the morning for Major Bilotta, it was seven in the evening for me. The sun, of course, was paying no attention to either of us. At this time of year it hovered far above the horizon twenty-four hours a day, so that it shone as brightly at midnight (by anyone's time) as at noon.

The amiable Bilotta did not let this contretemps bother him. "Our routine often gets a bit mixed up around here," he said genially. "We'll just change night into day for you, and schedule visits to start when it's your morning."

What more could a host do?

Friday the fifteenth of August—our time (it was still the evening of the fourteenth for Alfa)—"dawned" cloudy but warm, and we remained moored to the ice, spending the day on shore leave, arctic style.

After breakfast Nick, Bill Layman, and I started out with Major Bilotta for a tour of the station. It was a striking contrast with my solitary walk of the day before. The feeling of aloneness, of quietness, of cleanliness, was gone. Here the mark of man was everywhere. A fuel dump of barrels dropped by plane made an olive-drab blotch against the white snow. The same aquamarine melt ponds dotted the tops of the floes, but their pristine loveliness was marred by bits of trash and dirt.

Any dark-colored object dropped on the white snow cover absorbs so much heat in comparison to its surroundings that it soon melts its way deep into the ice. As we walked past the two-story radio antenna mast that dominated the camp, we noticed that the black rubber-coated wires laid out across the ice to the radio station had cut their way several feet down into the floe like hot knives slicing into butter.

The station consisted of about a dozen olive-drab buildings called Jamesway huts. They looked like the familiar quonset huts, but differed in that they were designed to be brought in piecemeal by plane and assembled with a minimum of time and effort. They were used variously as a mess hall, a recreation hall, quarters, and laboratories.

As we walked along I asked, "Why do you have ice blocks under all the huts?"

"Those aren't ice blocks," Bilotta replied with a smile. "That's where the ice used to be. When we brought the huts here last spring, the ice level was two or three feet higher. A lot has melted off since, except where the huts have insulated it from the sun."

Mounted on their pedestals of ice, the huts resembled sadly misshapen toadstools. It had been necessary for Bilotta's men to build wooden stairways to each door. As the summer progressed and the ice pedestals grew higher, the stairways gradually became longer and more rickety. Furthermore, a large melt pond seemed to have grown under each ladder so that quite a leap was required to clear it. Getting in and out of the huts was quite an adventure.

At the mess hall, an extra-large Jamesway which served as a sort of community center, we found Alfa's post office and made arrangements to take their outgoing mail with us. They were receiving mail from airplane drops, but no mail could go out until the autumn freeze once more allowed planes to land. Alfa's special postal cachet sported a polar bear and was labeled *Ice Skate 1958,* the code name for this scientific project. What better cachet for the letters we ourselves would post at Alfa?

In the mess hall we had coffee with Dr. Norbert Untersteiner, the Viennese-born senior civilian scientist, a tall, dark, impressive man in his late thirties, who spoke impeccable English. He was doing research work on the rate of growth and decay of the ice pack for the University of Washington.

Dr. Untersteiner volunteered to take us on a tour of the station's scientific plant, and led us out the back door of the mess hall. Here we saw our second and third polar bears of the week, but these two were butchered and hanging from a heavy post. "The boys shot them yesterday, not far from the station," Dr. Untersteiner explained. They looked huge, even as hanging pieces of meat. Their white furs were pegged out on boards nearby to dry.

"How's the meat?" Nicholson asked.

"Pretty strong," said Untersteiner wrily. Even in the outdoors, the gamy odor of the bear meat pervaded the air.

Untersteiner took us first to a laboratory where several young men were working on the "heat budget" of the Arctic. There has been much evidence in recent years that the Arctic is becoming warmer and that the area and thickness of the ice pack are diminishing. These trends are very gradual, however, and difficult to detect. The Alfa scientists were making careful measurements of the decreasing thickness of the floes as summer wore on, in hope of gathering evidence either to support or explode this theory.

In another part of the same laboratory were long plastic cylinders about two inches in diameter and as tall as a man that contained sample cores of the ocean floor, thousands of feet below us. These were obtained by a special device which was lowered through a hole cut in the floe to the bottom where it drove these cylinders like piles into the ocean floor. When these were recovered, they provided cross sections of the sediment of the ages from the undisturbed bottom of the Arctic Ocean.

"Not everyone agrees that this ocean has always been covered with ice, you know," said Untersteiner. I didn't know, and was greatly surprised. The fact that it was a deep ocean only thinly covered with ice had been enough for me to assimilate in the past three years.

Another part of the laboratory was taken up by the paraphernalia for a special camera which could take pictures of the ocean floor. The machine had been invented and built by the young men who were showing it to us, and they were obviously proud of it. Most of them were young graduate students, doing work either for the University of Washington or the Lamont Geological Laboratory of Columbia.

"Look," said one of them, pulling a photograph out of a file with evident relish. "We just got this one the other day."

The picture showed a large gray shape outlined in sharp shadow against a dim background. "What is it?" I asked.

"It's a boulder," he said, evidently surprised at my ignorance. "Over eight feet long. And this picture was taken by the flash of our floodlamp at a depth of over ten thousand feet."

Noting that the surrounding ocean floor in the photograph was apparently smooth, I asked: "How in the world did it get out here in the middle of the ocean?"

"That's a good question," said Untersteiner. "Possibly it got a ride on an ice island."

Untersteiner could see from my bewildered look that I didn't understand. "Well, the glaciers on certain arctic islands discharge into shallow bays fronting on the Arctic Ocean. In time, huge chunks of glacial ice, several miles across and 200 or so feet thick, break out of these bays and become a part of the polar ice pack. They are called ice islands. Naturally they contain glacial rocks and soil. When the islands drift out into the arctic basin, and thaws occur, the rocks may drop out to the bottom of the sea."

"Judging from the way it sits on top of the mud," I smiled in understanding, "this one couldn't have been there long."

"You're catching on," Untersteiner said. "In fact, we think this one's so recent that we're going to check the known ice-island tracks to try and find out which one dropped it."

As we left the laboratory Untersteiner laughed and said: "Of course, you can make other guesses as to how the boulder got there, but until a better one comes along, we'll go along with ours!"

Not far from the laboratory stood a derrick made of steel pipe, placed over a small hole cut through the ice, for the purpose of lowering scientific instruments into the sea. It was from this derrick that the bottom-sampling machine and the homemade deep-sea camera were let down on thin steel cables many thousand feet to the ocean floor.

"We also use it for a fishing hole," said Untersteiner. He went on to tell how they had caught only one fish, and that one under most unusual circumstances.

A baited line had hung in the ocean for weeks, with no success. One day a cold snap had made it necessary to pour alcohol around the hole in the ice to keep it from freezing over. An arctic fish, apparently fascinated with this hitherto unknown taste, had come sniffing around the hole. He remained long enough at the party to become stupefied, and was easily scooped up by the surprised scientific anglers. Untersteiner said he was about six inches long and identified as an ordinary herring.

About 50 yards from the laboratory hut stood a small white building about the size of a phone booth with an enormous lens in its roof. Untersteiner explained that this was a camera for photographing the northern lights; the continual sunlight and almost continual cloud cover of the arctic summer had put a stop to the program for the time being. He pointed out, however, that a great deal had been learned during the time the work had gone on.

There is apparently a definite relationship between this brilliant celestial phenomenon and events on the surface of the sun. This first came to the attention of scientists when it was observed that the frequency of sunspots seemed to have an effect on the frequency of the appearance of the northern lights. The theory now most widely accepted is that solar flares, cyclones of fiery gas on the sun's surface which are often associated with sunspots, send tongues of flame vast distances into the sun's atmosphere, raising the temperature in that atmosphere to several million degrees. This violent heat strips the hydrogen atoms in the sun's atmosphere of their single electron and somehow explodes the remaining proton into space. Roughly a day later these particles enter the magnetic field of the earth at velocities great enough directly or indirectly to excite the oxygen and nitrogen molecules of our atmosphere into giving off the familiar red-and-green glow we know as *aurora borealis*.

Dr. Untersteiner explained how the Geophysical Year program was obtaining correlated data on solar flares and aurora (in the southern hemisphere it is called *aurora australis*) from all over the world and hoped to pin down the relationship between the two more firmly. Naturally data from the atmosphere over the ice pack was a vital part of the pattern and could be gotten only from drifting stations such as Alfa.

We went on to another Jamesway hut, also used as a laboratory. Here the famous Latvian ice specialist, Dr. Arthur Assur, under contract to the US Army's Snow, Ice, and Permafrost Research Establishment, was investigating the strength of the arctic ice. He had equipment for testing its tensile and crushing strength, for taking core samples from various parts of the floe, and for measuring its temperature and salinity.

Untersteiner explained that Assur had done a lot of work exploring how much and just what sort of ice is required to support an airplane landing on it. Little did I realize that in a few months Assur's work was to become of vital interest to the *Skate,* as we attempted to determine how a submarine might actually break through the ice from beneath. But this gets ahead of our story.

Dr. Untersteiner took us back to the mess hall, where we had a sandwich and talked further about the work of the station. We could not help but be impressed by the devotion to learning which would lead a man of Untersteiner's ability and intelligence to isolate himself in this lonely and forlorn place for half a year. Dedicated as he was, it was apparent that he would be glad to go when the freeze came and planes could again land.

What motivates such men to this dedication? Certainly not desire for money or fame or even public recognition. It seems to me that it is their desire to observe, to catalogue, and to comprehend their world. They, like all of us, want to understand. But in these men the drive is strong enough to send them out to lonely places like Alfa, where they must beat their way through a summer swampland of ice and water to gain the knowledge for which they thirst.

Major Bilotta rejoined us and asked me if I'd like to make a telephone call back to the States. At first I thought he was joking, but he insisted that if I would come over to the radio station he would show me what he meant.

Before I said good-by to Untersteiner we made plans for a dinner that evening (*Skate* evening, not Alfa's). We would contribute steak, and someone at Alfa had saved a bottle of wine for an occasion.

This done, we made off across the ice swamp to the radio hut. Here was an array of up-to-date equipment and a cheerful Air Force operator in a gaudy fluorescent red shirt. It was the gayest color note I had yet seen at Alfa. The operator explained that if I would tell him whom I wanted to call he would take care of the details. I decided to start with the man who had sent the *Skate* to the North Pole: Rear Admiral Frederick Warder in New London.

Bilotta's operator swung into action. In clipped singsong tones, uttered with such rapidity that I wondered how anyone would ever understand him, he started calling for a reply from an amateur operator in the United States.

"Hello, any operator in the U.S., this is station KL7FLA near the North Pole calling."

Over and over went the call as Bilotta's operator changed his transmitting frequencies, attempting to make contact with some interested amateur over 2000 miles to the south.

We were not having much luck. Bilotta waved good-by and urged me to be patient—occasionally it took a bit of time.

My redshirted friend kept up his chant without any sign of wearing out. Untersteiner had told me there had been a good-sized solar flare a day or two before; apparently here was some of its handiwork. The electrically charged particles which come hurtling from the sun after a flare tend to break up the ionized layers in the earth's atmosphere against which redshirt was attempting to bounce his radio signal. Patience, I kept telling myself, patience.

Finally a faint voice came over our speaker. It was an amateur operator in Portland, Oregon. After much counting and talking back and forth, during which time frequencies were shifted several times in the hope of improving communication, we finally managed to receive our Portland friend fairly well. We asked him to patch his radio circuit into a long-distance telephone call to Admiral Warder in New London.

It wasn't until after I'd returned home that I learned how Admiral Warder received his call. He was at a formal luncheon along with several special guests. As the first course was being served, the telephone rang in the next room. A steward stepped out to answer it. In a few moments he was back with a quizzical look, beckoning for Lieutenant Thomson, the Admiral's aide, to come to the telephone.

Thomson is a young man who takes particular pride in remaining unruffled during the many crises that being aide to a busy man like Admiral Warder naturally brings. With an absolutely straight face he came back to the door and said: "Admiral Warder, telephone for you. It's Jim Calvert and he says he's calling from somewhere near the North Pole."

Toward the end of our conversation, which ran mostly to questions and assurances about families, the signal became weaker and weaker until we could scarcely hear. Finally the signal was lost altogether.

I wanted to place another call to Admiral Rickover in Washington, but although redshirt called forlornly for almost half an hour, we could find no more amateurs who could or would answer. Apparently the magnetic storm was blanking us out. I thanked my brilliantly garbed friend for all his effort. It had been no small task; he was perspiring and his voice was thoroughly hoarse.

Leaving the radio hut, I made my way back to the ship for a brief nap before dinner. I was awakened from a sound sleep by the phone buzzer. It was Guy Shaffer, the officer of the deck, who was standing his watch on the bridge just as if we were under way on the surface.

"Sorry to wake you up, Captain," Guy said, "but I think you'd better come up to the bridge. I'm certain this ice is starting to move."

I was dressed in an instant and on my way. All that I had read about swiftly closing leads that caught and crushed ships like pecans in a nutcracker flickered through my mind as I climbed the long ladder to the bridge. As I reached it, the dull boom of what sounded like distant thunder struck my ears.

Shaffer pointed toward the camp. "That pressure ridge has come up within the last hour," he said, referring to a long ridge of ice running dangerously near the main camp.

There had been no change in the weather; the temperature was still just at freezing, the wind gentle, and the sky lightly overcast. But somewhere in this great ocean of ice pressure was building up, pressure which was making itself felt here. We ran the risk of being squeezed to death in a slow but irresistible grip.

There was no doubt that our polynya was getting smaller. The motion was almost too slow to see, but if we sighted on certain edges of the polynya and watched them for a time it was apparent that our parking place was disappearing. Suddenly, with an ominous crack, a large chunk of floe ice perhaps 30 feet across broke loose not far from our bow and started drifting menacingly toward the ship.

How long would it be before we were in serious trouble? I didn't know, but I could only play it safe.

"Recall the crew, Guy," I said grimly. "We're going to have to leave." I realized this might take considerable time. Most of our civilian personnel were over at the station comparing notes with their Alfa counterparts. Many of the crew were visiting the station, and we had a considerable number of Alfa men on board visiting the *Skate*. (I very much regretted that during our visit the necessarily rigid security rules surrounding nuclear submarines prevented me from taking Dr. Untersteiner as my guest through the *Skate* because he was not a U.S. citizen.

But the word had not far to travel, and soon people were hurrying back to the ship from all directions. Dr. LaFond had run short of water sample bottles and he came clinking back encumbered by a huge tray of them obtained at the station. Boz Adkins, one of our electronics technicians, came back waving a pair of snowshoes he had won in a poker game.

My necessary but hasty decision disrupted all our plans. Charles Lasch, *Skate*'s chief yeoman, reminded me that all of our mail was still at the Alfa post office being cacheted with the special Ice Skate stamp.

Furthermore, since Alfa had no facilities for making ice cream, we had arranged to send over ten gallons of our best mixtures in exchange for some polar bear steaks, and this trade had yet to be consummated. Its negotiators were expressing great concern. I told them to hurry up and get the ice cream over while there was still time.

The ice cream was soon on its way in secondhand one-gallon tin cans. I sent notes over to Bilotta and Untersteiner apologizing for departing before dinner. The minutes ticked by, however, and still not all of us were back. I began to get more than a little worried. The faint distant boom of the ice furnished a sinister reminder of the danger of our situation.

Finally the polar bear steaks came aboard, wrapped carefully in wax paper. John Medaglia, our homegrown *Skate* philosopher and wit, took them as they were handed up from Bilotta's little motorboat.

"*Caramba!*" he exclaimed, "they were certainly generous with these things! Maybe they didn't want them so much." He put them down carefully on deck and called for a mess cook to come and get them. The dubious expression on Medaglia's face as he stood there, arms akimbo, looking at the enormous pile of steaks made me wonder just how they were likely to taste.

Finally the mail came on board in several sacks, and everyone was back but Walt Wittmann. He simply could not be found. Of course I had confidently told all hands we would leave about ten in the evening, so it was not Wittmann's fault, but I began to think that he might have to wait for the fall freezeup to leave.

The polynya was now down to half its former size. The lines with which we had been moored to the ice had been taken in and stowed, the iron stakes brought back on board, and the *Skate* moved to the center of the still unruffled but shrinking polynya.

At last we saw a tall lanky figure bounding across the ice and snow. It was Wittmann. He breathlessly explained that he had been deep in conversation with Dr. Assur and had not heard we were leaving.

We waved good-by to the men lining the edge of the lake—nearly all twenty-nine of them were there. The hatch was closed, and I went below to look everything over through the periscope before commencing our dive. Glancing around the edges of the polynya, at the men standing there, at the sparse pattern of huts and antennas behind them, I gave the order to Bill Cowhill to open the vents. As we slowly submerged I watched the men waving steadily from the edge of their lonely camp.

How well these men of Alfa embodied the meaning of Fridtjof Nansen when he said:

"Man wants to know, and when he ceases to do so he is no longer man."

CHAPTER 7

We traveled the night quietly, running 200 feet beneath the ice at 16 knots. I got up for breakfast next morning, having slept like a log. It was Saturday, the sixteenth of August—we had been in the ice pack for six days.

The breakfast table was full of high-spirited conversation about Alfa. Everyone seemed to have an experience he wanted to tell to the rest of us. Dave Boyd was enthusiastically describing how two young graduate students had been doing some skindiving under the ice floes. The rest of us shivered at the thought of going into that blue-black icy water, and Dave obviously thought us softies. He even felt rather guilty about all our comforts in the *Skate,* after having seen the rough-and-ready conditions on Alfa.

"We live entirely too well," said Dave earnestly. "How can you call this exploring when we sit down here with a fresh linen tablecloth and have eggs to order for breakfast?"

"I don't agree," I said. "In my opinion the greatest arctic explorer of them all was Nansen. And how did he travel? In style!"

I was referring to the way Nansen had outfitted the *Fram.* There were only thirteen men on board the ship, and they all lived in comfortable rooms surrounding a central wardroom (or saloon, as they called it) in which they all ate together. A special stove, combined with an elaborate insulating plan including quadruple doors and a triple-pane skylight, kept them warm and comfortable. Their food included the choicest delicacies that Norway could offer. Nansen even thought of their esthetic well-being: he installed a music box with changeable disks.

"Nansen wanted to get the information about the Arctic," I said, "but he didn't mind doing it in comfort if he could. I think he'd approve of us—and if he were alive now, he'd be right up here in a nuclear submarine."

"Could be," replied Dave dubiously, "but look what happened. He got so tired of his luxurious life in the *Fram* that he took off on foot for the North Pole, and spent the next year and a half slogging across the ice getting home without her!"

Dave had me there.

We had decided to return to the Lomonosov Ridge to survey it more thoroughly, proceeding directly across the polar basin to a point north of Greenland where we could intersect the huge underwater mountain chain. We planned to follow it back to the North Pole, crisscrossing it as we went.

As we sped toward the Lomonosov, we were still interested in surfacing whenever possible. It remained our primary mission and aim. However, with many miles yet to cover in our survey work, we were reluctant to slow down to search carefully for openings. I reasoned that even at 16 knots we might be able to find an occasional polynya if the officer of the deck watched carefully for streaks of open water and then swung the ship sharply, doubling back first to the right, then to the left. Slowing down as he turned, he would have a fairly good chance of passing under the same opening again.

Shortly after lunch, the *Skate* heeled sharply to starboard as she banked into a high-speed turn. Sitting in my room, I was nearly thrown from my chair. I wondered wildly what had gone wrong. Had we detected an iceberg ahead? Then, just as suddenly, the ship rocked to the other side. I now remembered—the new procedure. It must be getting its first trial. I hastened to the control center.

Bill Cowhill was officer of the deck. He was obviously enjoying these wild gyrations and the consternation they were causing. "Nice streak of open water," he exclaimed gleefully. "Hope we can find it again!"

In a few minutes the *Skate* had slowed to about 3 knots, and was easing her way through the same water she had recently sped through at 16.

"There it is!" called Walt Wittmann from the ice detector, "open water!" We had caught our polynya on the run. After plotting it out, we began to pump our way up. With surprising ease, and the confidence of experience, we soon reached the surface in our fifth lake of the week.

I climbed to the bridge to find the characteristic weather of the arctic summer: moist, cool air, just above freezing; a low, indolent breeze; a thin gray overcast. We inflated the rubber raft and sent the scientists on their way over to the ice for samples.

Wittmann and LaFond also took samples of the water at various depths. For 12 to 18 feet from the surface, polynya water is surprisingly fresh and warm; then a sharp transition occurs, and the water once more becomes salty and cold. There is a great difference in density between these two layers, and some objects that would sink in the light, warm fresh water float on the heavy, cold ocean water below. When we looked down, we could see tiny white arctic shrimp crawling along at the surface of this cold layer as if it were the bottom of the sea. The clarity of the water was startling. The shrimp were as clearly visible as though they had been floating in air.

The layer of fresh water comes from the melting of the ice around the edge of the polynya. Thus its depth is some indication of the age of the polynya. Ours had a layer of fresh water about 15 feet deep and was apparently several weeks old. The rounded and undercut edges of the ice tended to confirm this estimate.

Wittmann told us that the layer of fresh water in the polynya used to trouble the Eskimos and early northern explorers. A seal, when shot, sometimes has a tendency to sink. On occasion, a seal would sink through the dozen or so feet of fresh water at the top of the polynya, then float tantalizingly on the cold salt water, just out of reach of the hungry hunters. (Walt also mentioned, however, that the Eskimos had taken to attaching skin floats to their harpoons to hang onto their catch.)

I suddenly recalled an interesting phenomenon during two or

three of our surfacings, when I had kept the periscope up longer than usual. Just as the top of the periscope approached the fresh-water zone, my vision would become clouded. I couldn't understand what was happening until I realized that tiny organisms in the water were responsible. Nansen had discovered the same phenomenon. He found that in the summertime diatoms and algae, growing in the layer of fresh water at the top of the polynyas, sink to the bottom of this layer. These were what had clouded the periscope, and possibly they were what the shrimp in our polynya found so interesting. Then, of course, the seal eat the shrimp, and the bears eat the seal—and men eat the bears.

While Wittmann, LaFond, and I were talking on the deck, we were interrupted by a sudden commotion at the forward torpedo room hatch.

"Take it up! Get it out of here!" an unseen voice shouted. "I don't care what you do with it—just get rid of it!"

The voice belonged to Ray Aten. Soon the laughing face of John Medaglia appeared above the hatch. He was clutching the package of polar bear steaks we had been given the day before.

"We tried to get Aten to cook 'em," chuckled Medaglia, "but he took one look and threw us out of the galley. What's more, he said to get 'em out of his iceboxes and keep 'em out!"

Medaglia put the wax-paper package down on the deck and opened it. Heavy grease rolled off the fat-streaked meat; the gamy odor was overpowering.

"We're just not hungry enough," said Wittmann encouragingly. "These things are great when you are."

"Yeah," said Medaglia. "I just hope I *never* get that hungry." He dumped the steaks over the side.

They drifted down about 15 feet, and hung there suspended as though in midair.

"Look at that!" exclaimed Medaglia. "Even the ocean won't have 'em!"

Shortly before supper we dropped away from our polynya and continued on our way hoping to intersect the Lomonosov Ridge

during the night. About eleven, Art Molloy, our resident specialist on the ocean bottom, called me to the control center. "She's
beginning to show, now," he said, pointing to the sweeping
stylus of the fathometer. On the large traveling tape, an outline
of the Lomonosov foothills gradually appeared as we cruised
far above them at 16 knots. Within an hour we had crossed the
ridge of the chain, and had come about to head once more for
the Pole.

We spent the night and the next morning zigzagging over the
backbone of the range humped northward toward the top of the
world. Once more the fathometer needle drew dramatic profiles
of soaring crags and spectacular valleys as they passed beneath
us.

As the Lomonosov range nears the Pole it veers off slightly
to the left and passes perhaps 60 miles away on the Alaskan side.
Since we wanted to revisit the Pole to confirm some of our readings there, we left the ridge about noon on Sunday and headed
north. The memory of our difficulties in reaching the surface
near the Pole the Tuesday before was still vivid in our minds,
as we lazed along at 12 knots, on the lookout for a good spot
to try again.

By two o'clock we were within 50 miles of the Pole. Several
openings had appeared, but all were fairly small. Finally we
decided to try one of them, plotted it out, and stopped underneath it. Raising the periscope, I was dismayed to see deep-
hanging pressure ridges and black areas of heavy rafted ice all
around us. Why was it always this way at the Pole?

Determined to try again, we drifted up slowly and cautiously
through this forbidding canyon of ice. How simple this maneuver
could be at times—how nerve-wracking at others! As we rose, the
ice appeared to get closer and closer to the ship. I looked questioningly at Nick, but he assured me that—on paper—there was
nothing to worry about.

I peered out through the periscope at the evil-looking black
cliffs hemming in the *Skate* on three sides. "There's a big difference between getting your information from instruments and

looking through this scope and seeing what's *really* there!" I muttered.

When at last we were near enough to the surface to get the periscope out of the water, our situation was like that of our last attempt near the Pole all over again. The port side of the *Skate* was practically jammed against the ice and a brief glance around the polynya convinced me it was too small to surface in. It was scarcely more than 50 yards in diameter. Worse, I soon discovered, the stern of the ship was actually under a menacing shelf of ice. Undecided whether to remain awhile or move on immediately, I knew I must extricate the stern from this perilous position without delay.

"Starboard ahead one-third, port back one-third, left full rudder," I said, hoping to swing the stern clear of the obstruction.

Suddenly the ship vibrated from a heavy bump, followed by a hideous scraping noise astern.

"All stop!" I shouted. Everyone in the ship had the same dismaying thought: the rudder—it must have been the rudder! Abandoning all thought of remaining in this unlucky place, we flooded down and prayerfully tested our steering gear. With relief, we found that it seemed to operate normally. Then, one at a time, we tested the propellers. Again, apparently, all right.

After so many narrow brushes with the ice, it seemed hard to believe that we had finally hit it. It had probably been a gentle rap, yet the heavy grating vibration which had shaken the ship drove home to all of us that this sometimes innocent-looking blue-green substance covering and surrounding us was like cruel rock and, given the chance, could cripple our ship beyond repair.

As we pressed on for the Pole, the Arctic, as though it had inflicted its final persecution upon us for the time being, suddenly opened up. Only 40 miles from the North Pole we found the largest polynya of our cruise—nearly half a mile in diameter. We surfaced in it easily, with the feeling of release from unbearable confinement. It was clear that the North Pole area did have some large lakes after all. Common sense—and Walt Wittmann—had told us so, but experience is a powerful influence.

As soon as the hull was above water, Bill Layman and his men ran aft to examine the rudder. The electric-light fixture that was built into its top was gone—scraped off as cleanly as though by a knife. But the rudder itself was undamaged.

As Bill was working back at the rudder a seal poked his head up inquisitively about 30 yards away, but came no nearer this strange black monster in his domain. It must have puzzled him considerably, for he bobbed up and down gazing at us for several minutes. Apparently he had no fear of the men—probably because he had never seen any.

We flooded down and continued north. By eleven that evening, the *Skate* was back at the North Pole for the second time in a week.

"It took submarines a while to find their way up here," cracked John Medaglia, "but now they've started regular service!" He was referring to the fact that, counting the *Nautilus*, there had been three submarine visits to the Pole in the last two weeks.

We took careful readings of the depth, transparency, and temperature of the water. Zane Sandusky made detailed readings of his inertial equipment. We then pulled two miles away from the Pole and made a trip around the roughly 12-mile circle in one hour, probably the fastest round-the-world trip ever made. The real purpose was not to set a record, but to enable Art Molloy to take soundings in the vicinity of the Pole in order to gather data for a detailed chart of the area.

I had not given up the idea of surfacing right at the Pole. During our cruise around the world we kept a hopeful eye on the ice machine. No opening.

We closed in for one last check at the Pole itself before departing. When we were almost precisely at the spot we saw a very encouraging stretch of apparently open water. Experience had made us adept at plotting its outline. We were soon on our way up. Everything looked fine through the periscope until we got close to the surface. I gulped in astonishment and alarm. The surface of the lake was frozen solid. I could see cracks in this ice, and light penetrated it quite well, but it was there.

This had been our constant fear—that we might smash blindly into ice when we thought we had open water above us. The ship was not prepared for any contact with it. Even if we had the periscope withdrawn and even if there were no damage to the sail, our delicate radio antennas, upon which rested all our hope of contact with the outside world, trailed vulnerably aft from masts up there. To crash through even thin ice would mangle these delicate devices and leave us mute.

"Take her down, ice above!" I snapped quickly to Bill Cowhill. He immediately opened the vent on the negative tank (a special tank designed to enable the *Skate* to take on additional weight quickly in an emergency) and thousands of pounds of water rushed into it almost instantaneously. First hesitating, then dropping as though she had been yanked with a wire, the *Skate* sank away from danger above.

I turned angrily to Al Kelln. "Didn't you show ice on that machine of yours?" I asked.

Al looked completely mystified, and beckoned to me to come and look. The tape clearly showed open water.

By this time Bill had blown his negative tank and regained normal buoyancy. We set our course away from the Pole. We concluded soberly that the echo from thin ice and open water could look much the same. But what a difference it would make to us!

We returned down the spine of the Lomonosov, picking out several now-familiar peaks as we retraced our path and turned toward the Greenland–Spitsbergen Strait. We were headed for home.

As the great ice drift of the polar sea moves toward the channel between Greenland and Spitsbergen, it jams millions of tons of ice against the northern coast of the two islands. The pack in this region is rafted, heavy-packed, and treacherous. We were anxious not only to survey it from underneath, but also, if possible, to surface in it, to demonstrate once more our mastery of the technique.

For many hours it looked as if our plans were doomed to disappointment. Walt Wittmann's ice log recorded the depressing story:

"August 19 . . . a strong compaction area . . . deepest pressure ridges we have yet seen. . . . No trace of an opening in the past fifty miles. . . ."

Then, on the evening of the nineteenth, we shot under a small but usable opening. Without a moment's hesitation, officer of the deck Pat Garner threw the rudder over and sent coffee cups crashing to the deck as the *Skate* heeled sharply to starboard. Skillfully the veteran crew worked the ship to the surface. We had come up safely for the ninth time in our ten days in the ice pack.

Already we were passing out of the arctic climate, with its almost constant overcast. Here the sun shone brightly through a mackerel sky, brightening the pale azure glints of the melt ponds and the ermine of the snow and turning the protruding ice edges to flashing diamonds. The Arctic was putting on her most dazzling face for her good-by.

As we sank out of our last lake I felt genuinely sorry. I was sure I was seeing the Arctic for the last time, and I had come to love it.

All day Wednesday we streaked on a southerly course past the northeast corner of Greenland. The ice machine, which had lost most of its popularity as a source of entertainment, made a strong comeback. As openings in the ice became more and more frequent, a weight seemed to lift slowly from the ship.

Although our confidence in our ability and in our ship had grown with every day we had spent under the ice, there had been little or none of the fooling or horseplay that so often lightens duty aboard ship. We had been engaged in a grim and serious business that just hadn't allowed much time or opportunity for it.

But now I walked into the control center to witness a sight that made me realize the pressure was vanishing. The stocky figure of John Medaglia was the center of attention. He was crouching over, grasping an imaginary periscope, and twirling around and around.

"Easy now, easy now . . . bring her up slowly . . . *s-l-o-w-l-y*. . . . Saaay, this ice is really *close!* Are you *sure* we've got enough room here, Nicholson?"

Medaglia's all-too-expert imitation was getting a tremendous laugh. I stole away so as not to disturb the fun.

By six-thirty in the evening, Walt Wittmann announced that he thought we were completely clear of the ice. The ice detector had shown nothing but the thin black line of open water for several miles. I brought the *Skate* to periscope depth at the normal speed of 4 or 5 knots for the first time since before we had approached Prins Karls Forland on the ninth of August. I raised the periscope to find a gently rolling swell. The sun was setting in a burst of rose-colored clouds, and the ice was only a faint white line to the north.

High-pressure air hissed into the tanks, and the *Skate* rolled to the surface, bone in her teeth, with a perceptible swagger. Soon she was dashing along at 15 knots, burying her nose in the swell and then shaking herself high and free with the white water cascading gracefully from her bow. It was as though she was exultant to be in the deep swells of the Atlantic again, free of the confining ice of the Arctic.

After several radio messages were sent, we submerged once more and set off for Bergen, Norway, where we had been ordered to proceed when we had left the Arctic.

As soon as we dove, I took a walk back into the engine room. I can never describe the feeling I had that evening about the *Skate*. The affection men feel for ships and machinery that serve them well in time of need can never be explained. It is a totally irrational thing, but that does not make it less real.

As I walked between the gleaming rows of pipes and turbines

and heard the deep-throated throb of power running through those turbines to our propellers, a shiver of awe ran up and down my back. This machinery, upon whose integrity our very lives depended, had never faltered, never missed a beat. How could I help feeling it was a living presence and knew how I felt?

Bill Layman was on watch in the maneuvering room. The expression on his face told me I didn't have to explain what I had been thinking.

"It's a good ship, Captain," Bill said with simple finality. For taciturn Bill, that was truly outspoken.

I shall never forget our entry into Bergen. Hazy sunlight gave a gauzy radiance to the blue-black water and stark granite of the fjords. Waving families stood by story-book cottages, resplendent in red, yellow, and blue paint, that lined the water's edge. All had Norwegian flags flying proudly in the yard, and one family even fired a skyrocket in salute. With deep pride I recalled that just sixty-five years before, Nansen and his sturdy *Fram* had departed from these same fjords on much this sort of day. And the same bright cottages and flags that now welcomed us had wished him godspeed as he started on his voyage to the north.

A few days later, in Oslo, a ceremony was held at the museum which now houses the *Fram* as a national shrine for the Norwegian people. We placed a spray of flowers at the base of Nansen's statue, and a bronze plaque bearing the emblem of the *Skate* was placed on board the *Fram* commemorating our visit. Bronze plaques from the *Skate* are mounted in many places in America and Europe, but none give me more personal satisfaction than the one aboard this small wooden ship.

It added much to this occasion to have the famous arctic flyer Colonel Joe Fletcher on hand for the ceremony. Colonel Fletcher very kindly gave me his personal copy of a first edition of Nansen's *Farthest North*. Folded into one of the volumes is a well-worn chart. On it, in a fine and graceful hand, appears the signature ·Nansen.

As the days went by, messages of congratulation for the *Skate* poured in from many places. They meant a great deal to us, but actually we already had all the reward we wanted. We knew that we had accomplished what we had set out to do—that both the crew and the ship had met the challenge set them. Not only had we developed new skills, for which there were no precedents, but we had proved to ourselves that we could do it.

But as honors and congratulations for the *Skate* came in, I thought once more of the fjord at Bergen. At its bottom, deep in its shadowy water, lies rusting, largely forgotten, the hulk of another submarine that once sailed proudly for the North Pole —the *Nautilus* of Sir Hubert Wilkins. We had talked to many of his friends in Bergen and Oslo; one of them, Dr. Odd Dahl, had given me a copy of Wilkins' *Under the North Pole*. This was a book that Wilkins wrote before he went on his *Nautilus* expedition in 1931, telling what his plans and ideas were. It was one of the ways by which he had raised money for the expedition.

I was unable to put this book down until I finished it. Here was a work, written when I was eleven years old, which again and again forecast accurately what we had just experienced.

And how had it ended? I thought again of the hulk of the *Nautilus* beneath the waters near Bergen. I wanted to do something to express my feeling of admiration for the spirit and vision of this man. I drafted a message to Sir Hubert, whom I had never met:

REQUEST PASS TO SIR HUBERT WILKINS X THE EXPERIENCES OF THIS SUMMER FOLLOWED BY CONVERSATIONS WITH YOUR OLD ASSOCIATES IN BERGEN AND OSLO HAVE LEFT US DEEPLY AWARE OF THE ACCURACY OF YOUR INSIGHT AND VISION IN REGARD TO THE USE OF SUBMARINES IN THE ARCTIC X THE MAJORITY OF YOUR AIMS AND PREDICTIONS OF NEARLY THIRTY YEARS AGO WERE REALIZED THIS SUMMER X THE MEN OF THE SKATE SEND A SINCERE SALUTE TO A MAN WHO HAS MANY TIMES SHOWN THE WAY

As we were crossing the Atlantic on our way to a special homecoming welcome in Boston, we received a reply from Wilkins:

SIR HUBERT WILKINS SINCERELY APPRECIATES THE MESSAGE FROM THE MEN OF THE SKATE AND EXTENDS TO THEM HEARTY CONGRATULATIONS UPON THEIR SKILLFUL AND EFFICIENT ACCOMPLISHMENT OF A MEASURE WHICH NO DOUBT WILL LEAD TO NEW AND FAR REACHING DEVELOPMENTS IN SCIENCE ECONOMICS AND DEFENSE

On September 22 we arrived in Boston amid the roar of helicopters and the tooting of tugboats. While we were still in the harbor, a launch bearing Dennis Wilkinson and Admiral Rickover came out to meet the *Skate*.

It was the will and imagination of these two men that had made our venture possible. Naturally I was glad to see them. But as the *Skate* drew near to her berth I could see in the crowd on the pier the softly smiling face of the one who had had the hardest job of all—she who had the courage to remain at home and wait.

PART III

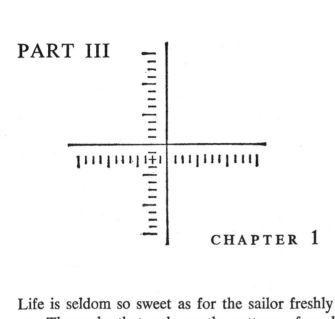

CHAPTER 1

Life is seldom so sweet as for the sailor freshly home from the sea. The cycles that make up the patterns of our lives—night and day, winter and summer, hope and realization—all seem to be echoed in the cycle of the long sea voyage and the return home. Perhaps this explains, in part, the fascination of the sea.

Never had our hundred-year-old white frame house in Mystic seemed so attractive, and never had the conversation and problems of our three children seemed so interesting. Thoughts of the Arctic and the *Skate* faded into the background in a round of family activities.

But a few weeks after our return, on the eighteenth of October, I received a visitor who rekindled all my interest in the Arctic. Sir Hubert Wilkins came to spend a day on the *Skate*. The old explorer was still vigorous and alert, and enthusiastic and curious about all the intricacies of the nuclear submarine. The clear, kind eyes and firm grasp were those of a younger man.

All morning, while the *Skate* lay peacefully moored at the Electric Boat dock, Sir Hubert and I discussed the 1931 voyage of the *Nautilus*. Before our conversation was over Sir Hubert had done a lot of reminiscing about his full and fruitful life.

Born on a ranch in Australia, he had seen the often-tragic results of ignorance of what the weather might bring. A desire to bring accurate long-range weather forecasting to the world became for Wilkins one of the strongest motivations of a long polar career. As a young man he accompanied Vilhjalmur Stefansson on his explorations of the Canadian archipelago from 1913 to 1916, serving as photographer and as one of Stefansson's most trusted assistants. Wilkins left the expedition before its termination and joined the Australian forces fighting in Europe, where he reached the rank of captain and received the Military Cross. In 1921 he sailed toward the Antarctic with the famous Ernest Shackleton, who just a few years before had electrified the world by returning alive with all of his men after his ship *Endurance* had been crushed and sank in the antarctic Weddell Sea, a thousand miles from civilization. The 1921 expedition ended, however, when Shackleton died of a heart attack during the voyage south.

Wilkins was the first to fly completely across the Arctic Ocean, in 1928, when he and Ben Eielson, employing a Great Circle Route, crossed from Alaska to Spitsbergen, passing over the North Pole en route. For this flight Wilkins received a knighthood. Then, the same year, he commanded the Wilkins–Hearst Antarctic Expedition, adding to his honors by exploring new regions at the other end of the earth. He became known as the foremost polar aviator of his day.

His attention turned, however, to the beguiling field of the submarine. As far back as 1915, Stefansson in his colorful fashion compared exploring the Arctic by air with trying to learn what was in a garden by flying over it. He convinced Wilkins that detailed knowledge about the vast ocean that covered the top of the world could best be obtained from a submarine passing underneath its ice. In 1930 Wilkins began a serious campaign to obtain a submarine for arctic exploration.

From the first he ran into every imaginable obstacle. Submarines and everything connected with them are crushingly expensive; they are the playthings of governments, not of individuals. However, Wilkins would not give up. His persistence finally paid off when he made an arrangement with the United States Shipping Board to turn over to him an old Navy submarine, the former 0–12. But his acquisition was not an unmixed blessing, for the ship was badly run down by thirteen years of service and was considered thoroughly obsolete.

Furthermore, Wilkins was neither a submarine operator nor designer. He knew that he needed the services of both. He went to the firm of Lake and Danenhower—both illustrious names in the underwater field. Simon Lake was a pioneer submarine inventor, while Sloan Danenhower was an Annapolis graduate who had become an experienced submarine officer before going into business with Lake.

Lake and Danenhower agreed to take the old 0–12 and make her into a polar submarine. Lake would design the necessary modifications and Danenhower would operate the ship when completed. It was Wilkins' hope to create a vessel that would make possible careful examination of the Arctic Ocean. It would have room for a scientific laboratory and its staff, plus the facilities which would allow an expedition to remain comfortably in the Arctic as long as desired. Sir Hubert envisioned a twentieth-century *Fram,* built to go under the water rather than drift in the ice.

Instead, Lake and Danenhower proceeded to build a fantastic contrivance containing many of the devices, practical and crackpot, that Simon Lake had dreamed up during his long career. (As early as 1898 he had written an article for the New York *Journal* entitled "To the North Pole in a Submarine Boat with Dynamite to Blow Holes in the Ice.")

The submarine was outfitted with a hydraulically cushioned bowsprit, a jackknifing periscope, a hydraulically cushioned guide arm to allow the submarine to ride under the ice in the fashion of a trolley car, and three drills to bore air holes through the ice while the ship was moored beneath the pack.

Sir Hubert objected to most of these gimcracks, but under the terms of the contract Lake and Danenhower had the right to decide what equipment was necessary for safe operation of the submarine. They were the experts.

Meanwhile Sir Hubert was busily engaged in the arduous task of raising money for the expedition. From the beginning his wealthy friend Lincoln Ellsworth had agreed to help, but more money was needed. Wilkins approached William Randolph Hearst, with whom he had been recently fortunately affiliated in the Antarctic, and Hearst consented to help support the expedition. The Texas Oil Company also agreed to help. Wilkins also went on a lecture tour, and even compiled a book, written by himself and other members of the expedition and called *Under the North Pole,* to raise money. Finally, Sir Hubert put much of his own money into the effort.

Eventually the work was completed and the ship was re-christened *Nautilus* in March 1931. Jean Jules Verne, grandson of the man who had conceived the first *Nautilus,* was present. Lady Wilkins, Sir Hubert's bride of less than two years, chris-tened the ship by pouring a bucket of ice over its bow.

In June the submarine sailed from Provincetown. The de-parture was at eleven o'clock at night to avoid sailing on Friday —which the superstitious crew considered unlucky. But this precaution was of no avail. Much effort had gone into installing harebrained gadgets and little into seeing that the ship was sound in her vitals. Within ten days, serious mechanical trouble had the little submarine wallowing in the trough of the sea and waiting for the American battleship *Wyoming,* which had agreed to tow her to Ireland. From there she was towed to the British Admiralty dockyard at Devonport, England, where a full month of fundamental repair work was required to fit the ship for sea.

One important member of the *Nautilus* expedition was not aboard during this transatlantic odyssey. Dr. Harald Sverdrup, a distinguished Norwegian oceanographer, had agreed to go along as senior scientist. In Sverdrup, Wilkins had chosen a man almost good enough to make up for what his other two experts lacked. Sverdrup was a respected scientist who had previously spent several years in the Arctic with Roald Amundsen's *Maud* expedition. He was later to become head of the Scripps Institute of Oceanography at La Jolla, California. Sverdrup was a staunch advocate of the use of submarines for scientific research in the Arctic. He later gave Waldo Lyon much encouragement and inspiration in his pioneer work with the submarine in the 1940s. Dr. Sverdrup died in 1957, unfortunately just too early to see his predictions borne out in the polar voyages of nuclear submarines.

In 1931, Sverdrup had gone ahead to Bergen to make final arrangements and there he awaited the *Nautilus* as she made her slow and painful way across the ocean. Sverdrup knew well the area around Spitsbergen where Wilkins planned to enter the polar sea. The *Skate* used the same spot twenty-seven years later, and for the same reasons: this is the point where the Gulf Stream pushes the arctic ice pack farthest north.

Sverdrup knew that if the *Nautilus* wished to take advantage of the arctic summer, with its frequent polynyas and mild weather, she should be at Spitsbergen by late June. His anxiety increased during the summer as delay after delay occurred. Finally, on the first of August, the *Nautilus* sailed forlornly into Bergen. Wilkins was determined not to give up, and Sverdrup, though discouraged at the lateness of the season, stood by him.

Sir Hubert's primary purpose in the *Nautilus* expedition was to establish means of accurate and permanent weather observations in the arctic ice pack. He intended to demonstrate that a permanent base for scientists could be established on the ice, and that this base could be supported by a submarine. (Remember that Storkerson's earlier camp on the ice had lasted only a short time, and that this was twenty-seven years before the *Skate* visited Station Alfa).

He also intended to take soundings, obtain water samples, observe arctic currents, measure air and water temperatures, attempt radio communication with civilization, study the formation of the pack and measure the amount of light transmitted through the ice, and determine the effect of arctic operations on a submarine. (These were the almost exact aims of the *Skate* in 1958.)

So, even though the season was late, Wilkins pressed on, determined to accomplish as much scientific work as possible. On the nineteenth of August the *Nautilus* passed Prins Karls Forland. Late that afternoon she entered the outskirts of the pack and began to thread her way, on the surface, among the blocks of ice.

It was Sir Hubert's intention not to run below and clear of the ice, as *Skate* was later to do, but to be in contact with it at all times, sliding underneath it as a sled would slide over it. For this purpose the topside had been made smooth and sledlike. Sir Hubert knew about the pressure ridges under the ice but counted on sledding under or around them.

It must be recalled that Sir Hubert had no mechanism to tell him whether water or ice was overhead, no source of power which would enable him to remain submerged, no means of keeping his air breathable indefinitely. He realized that the *Nautilus* would have to take advantage of every opportunity to reach the surface. The plan was for the ship to slide underneath the ice with positive buoyancy, so that she would pop automatically to the surface whenever she encountered a polynya. If this scheme failed, one of Simon Lake's drills was to be used to bore through the ice and obtain air for the men and the diesel engines.

These plans were not formulated at a time when the submarine had been tempered by many years of use in peace and war, or freed from dependence on the atmosphere by nuclear power. Rather, the ship was designed and the trip planned in the technically murky atmosphere which surrounded submarining in 1931, redolent with the recent memories of the S–51 and S–4 disasters.

Sir Hubert must truly have been, as his friends have often stated, a man who did not understand the meaning of fear.

But the men associated with him did. Lacking the cohesive

organization of a military ship and skippered by Danenhower, whose administration, in Wilkins's kindest understatement, ". . . was not always of a character conducive to maximum efficiency," the men simply became frightened.

The rickety old submarine had broken down repeatedly all the way across the Atlantic, and the men understandably had no stomach for venturing under the ice where the ship would have to perform reliably all the time. They wanted to go home.

But the fearless determination of Wilkins was not to be put down. The *Nautilus* pressed northward in the drifting block-and-brash ice in the teeth of a fierce gale. Finally it was decided that the ship was ready for a dive. The corpulent Danenhower shuffled along topside for a last-minute check. He looked into the water astern and then looked again. The stern diving planes were gone. Simply missing. This is roughly equivalent to going out to start your car and finding that the steering wheel has been stolen. It was an unexpected and devastating blow.

Sir Hubert told me something which he never put in writing but has been a poorly kept secret for years. The stern planes of the *Nautilus* did not simply fall off; they were sabotaged, possibly by members of the crew. Apparently in Bergen someone had gone into the water and damaged the planes in such a way that after a few days at sea they would be gone.

But whoever hoped thus to halt the voyage had not reckoned with Wilkins. He ordered the ship to go under the ice without the use of stern planes. The ship, he maintained, would be sledding under the ice and would not need them.

The weather, however, became too rough for attempting to submerge, and the *Nautilus* continued to press northward through the broken ice at the edge of the pack. By August 28 they had been among the ice floes ten days and had reached a latitude of nearly 82 degrees. This was roughly 100 miles north of Spitsbergen—farther north than any ship had ever been under her own power. Still they had not made a dive. Only Dr. Sverdrup had accomplished any of the tasks planned for the expedition; ever since they had passed Prins Karls Forland he had been hard at work sounding the uncharted ocean, taking water and bottom samples, and making scientific observations of every kind.

On August 31 the wind finally abated. Wilkins was determined to try sliding the *Nautilus* under a floe if only to test whether the method was practical. By now, however, the large ice drill had become jammed in a partially raised position and could not be lowered. In addition to all her other handicaps, the *Nautilus* now had a carbon steel spur several inches long jutting out of the supposedly smooth upper deck.

But under they went. Danenhower trimmed the ship down by the bow but did not flood her main ballast tanks, thus retaining much of her positive buoyancy. Then, after backing away from a convenient ice floe, the little *Nautilus* went at it like an enraged bull. The results were spectacular. The bow hit the ice with a crash, ducked under, and started to slide. Then the drill began to scrape into the ice, and inside the thin hull it sounded as though the demons of hell were attempting to demolish the ship. Finally she stalled, propellers thrashing, half under the floe like a floating log caught under a rock on the shore. Danenhower backed her out and tried again. Again the *Nautilus* stalled with her bow under the ice and her stern in the air.

Danenhower himself really did much to defeat the attempt to submerge beneath the ice. He insisted on keeping the *Nautilus* trimmed with about thirty tons of positive buoyancy; this, combined with the stuck drill, prevented her from acting like a submarine—or even like an inverted sled. But he was the submarine expert, and Wilkins could not argue with him on this point.

On one of these abortive slides, Sir Hubert managed to obtain some remarkable motion pictures through glass ports in the superstructure. In these the underside of the ice can be clearly seen; the jump of the camera, as the *Nautilus* lurched forward dragging the stuck drill through the ice, adds to the dramatic effect.

After a few more tries, Wilkins was convinced that even his

iron will could not force the *Nautilus* to do more. He sent a radio message stating that the arctic cruise was over. The *Nautilus* returned to Bergen.

There, in late September, the crew was paid off and Wilkins, who had put more than $250,000 of his own money into the project, was left practically penniless. Under the terms of his contract with the Government, it was his responsibility to dispose of the submarine in such a way that she could never be used for war. The fjord at Bergen is deep—over 600 feet near the docks. The *Nautilus* was towed out into the still water and her valves opened. Down she went and there she remains, in the fjord that saw the ships of the Vikings return from conquest and exploration, saw medieval vessels of the Hanseatic fleet arrive laden with riches, saw Nansen's *Fram* depart for the Arctic in 1893, and saw the *Skate* return in 1958.

Was the expedition a total failure? By no means. Much of the scientific information Sverdrup obtained during the two-week period that the *Nautilus* was in the edges of the pack remained the best available until the cruises of the nuclear *Nautilus* and *Skate*.

There were, undeniably, certain circuslike aspects to the expedition, but these were resorted to only in order to raise money for a privately financed expedition of a sort usually attempted only with total or substantial government financing. Over-all, it was eloquent testimony to the stalwart determination of a remarkable man.

Sir Hubert remained aboard the *Skate* for lunch, and afterward we briefly discussed her voyage north. I felt a little ashamed telling him about the wealth of mechanical devices we possessed —the finest that money could buy. Everything which for him had proved balky or useless had, after twenty-seven years of intensive submarine development, either been replaced by something far better or improved beyond recognition.

But Sir Hubert took all this progress in stride—he had the wisdom to know that it is courage and imagination which matter most, that in the fullness of time the gadgets are likely to come which will enable the dream to be fulfilled.

"Now that you have everything you need to do the job," said the old explorer suddenly, "you must go in the wintertime."

I was startled but knew what he meant. Every bit of submarine exploration in the Arctic had been done in summer, when polynyas are abundant. In winter they would be frozen over and open water nonexistent or very difficult to locate.

"You haven't really opened the Arctic Ocean for scientific investigation—" Sir Hubert went on, "or military or commercial use, for that matter—if you merely demonstrate what you can do in the summertime."

"How much open water do you think we'd find in the winter?" I asked.

"Oh, you'd probably find some," he replied, "but it'd be scarce."

"Not much use in going if we can't get to the surface," I said dubiously.

"I think you can," he replied. "Maybe you'll have to bore a hole, maybe blast. I don't know—but you'll find a way."

Then a long sigh escaped him, and he sat for some time with a faraway look and a half-smile. I'm sure he found it hard to face the fact that the years were past when he could take active part in such an adventure.

A week or so after the visit of this gallant man, I received a letter from him, graciously thanking us for our hospitality and containing this advice:

I . . . have given considerable thought to the idea of a winter expedition. You must attempt to bring this about. Do not be discouraged by apathy and resistance, press for it. . . .

On the first of December I learned of his death from a heart attack.

CHAPTER 2

In late January, Nancy and I drove to Hanover, New Hampshire, where I gave a talk on the cruise of the *Skate* at Dartmouth College. Only while attending a post-lecture reception did I fully realize to whom I had been talking. I had known that Vilhjalmur Stefansson was a member of the Dartmouth faculty, but many other arctic specialists were also there: Professor Trevor Lloyd, an international authority on arctic geography and weather; Dr. Lincoln Washburn, an arctic geological expert; and Dave Nutt, a Dartmouth research associate who has done much arctic research work in his schooner *Blue Dolphin*. I'm afraid that if I'd known all these men made their home at Dartmouth, I would not have dared speak a word. However, if I made any errors, they were too courteous to point them out.

The next morning I visited Dartmouth's huge Baker Memorial Library where, in a special section, is housed the Stefansson collection of arctic literature. (This, incidentally, is the second largest such collection in the world. The largest is in the Institute of the Arctic at Leningrad—evidence of the deep Russian interest in this region.) There I found Stefansson himself at work amidst a mountain of papers. His rugged build and vigorous demeanor belied his seventy-nine years. His remarkable mind is still as keen as ever and, with the help of his attractive and energetic wife Evelyn (an outstanding arctic scholar in her own right), he applies himself daily to writing and to maintaining his vast correspondence with people all over the world.

Born in Canada of Icelandic parents, he has long championed the Arctic as a region for expansion and economic development. In his best-known book, *The Friendly Arctic,* Stefansson maintains that the north is not a barren, frozen waste, but actually a land of plenty for those who will adapt themselves to it rather than attempt to maintain their temperate-zone habits. At the same time, it must be admitted that Stefansson was probably better equipped personally than almost any other white man at adapting to the Arctic. He was a magnificent hunter who learned the trick of thinking as the animals thought; once he got his quarry in the sights of his gun, he almost never missed. He lived well and gained weight in circumstances where other men starved and froze.

He remains one of the great authorities on the northlands and it is heartwarming to find him, in his old age, in a place where his priceless collection of arctic books and pamphlets has a good home and where his work and significance are understood and appreciated.

I was interested to learn that Stefansson, one of the few white men who can build as good a snow house as the Eskimos, constructs one every now and then on the Dartmouth campus!

As I came into his office, the veteran explorer riffled through his desk drawer and found a thin piece of paper which he handed to me. It was a copy of the message I had sent Sir Hubert Wilkins from Europe. Sir Hubert had passed on this copy to Stefansson with the note:

WRONG ADDRESSEE—SHOULD HAVE BEEN SENT TO YOU.
—W.

The death of Wilkins—nine years his junior—had been a blow for Stefansson, and he talked for a time of his admiration and affection for his old friend. We discussed my conversations with Wilkins at length, especially Wilkins' suggestion that we go to the Arctic in winter.

Stefansson gazed out over the snow-covered campus. "He would, of course," he said. "He always wanted to press into the thick of things."

"What do you think about it?" I asked.

"You'll find it a lot different from what you saw last August," Stefansson replied.

The first thing we would have to take into consideration, he told me, would be the difference in weather. The summertime Arctic is comparatively mild. Temperatures stay very close to 32 degrees Fahrenheit and the winds are gentle. The air is humid; the sky is almost always overcast. The ice floes are covered with melt ponds and the general atmosphere is one of a cloudy but unexpectedly warm winter day in the temperate zone when ice and snow seem on the verge of thaw.

Arctic winter is nothing like this. The temperature average in winter over the Polar Sea is a frigid 30 below. The winds are stronger, with occasional severe gales. The melt ponds are gone. The floes present an unbroken face of white snow and glittering ice. The atmosphere is bleak and hostile.

The lowest temperatures of the arctic winter occur in January, February, and March, and just as the coldest hour of the night is about 3 A.M., so the coldest part of the Arctic winter is in March. That month marks the climax of conditions resulting from the long absence of the sun. Naturally, at this time the ice is at its heaviest.

Stefansson also talked about the light in the winter Arctic. In the planning of our August trip this had never been considered, since we knew we would have full daylight twenty-four hours a day while we were in the ice pack. But from September until March the sun leaves the Arctic to darkness. This darkness is not total everywhere. The amount of available light depends to a large extent on distance from the Pole. For example, where the northernmost Eskimos live (about 700 nautical miles from the Pole) the sun is below the horizon for only a bit more than sixteen weeks of each year—and of these sixteen, five have a useful twilight. Such twilight is very important; during much of the winter night the sun is close enough to the horizon to give almost as much light as though it were risen.

The moon also provides considerable illumination. At the Pole the moon rises when it is half full and remains in the sky until it is on the wane and half gone. The sparkling winter air and the highly reflective snow combine to make the moon a much more significant source of light than in ordinary latitudes.

One subject remained to be discussed. In the winter, I asked Stefansson, could a submarine hope to find open water in which to surface?

That, he said, was a hard question to answer. He thought open water as such would be very scarce. But water with thin ice—that might be a different matter. He went on to explain that leads are opened by the movement of the ice floes, but the intense cold freezes them over quickly, and they never get a chance to open into the familiar polynyas of the summer.

"How fast do they freeze over?" I asked.

"It depends on the wind and temperature. In still air and temperatures at thirty below zero, the sea water will freeze six inches the first day, four more inches the second day, and so on. In a week you'd have a foot and a half or so. Do you think," Stefansson asked, "you could break that much ice with the *Skate?*"

I said, in all honesty, that I had no idea.

"Let me show you something," said Stefansson, getting up from his desk and reaching for a copy of *The Friendly Arctic*. He thumbed through it briefly. "Here. Read this," he said, handing me the open book.

Stefansson and two companions were in the middle of a trek across the ice between Alaska and Banks Island. They were more than 100 miles from land, camped near a recently frozen lead. They were suddenly awakened from sleep by the barking of their dogs. Then they too heard the noise that had upset the dogs. It was the blowing of whales. A school of beluga whales were swimming along the lead, breaking the ice as they passed:

> It was interesting to see the six- or eight-inch ice bulge and break as they struck it with the hump of their backs. A moment after the noise of breaking ice would come the hiss of the spouting whale and a column of spray.

"If the beluga whales could do it, why not the *Skate?*" said the smiling Stefansson.

Before I left Hanover Dr. Stefansson gave me a copy of *The Friendly Arctic*. On the flyleaf he wrote:

To Calvert of the Skate from Stefansson of the Sledge with special reference to the achievements of the Wilkins's and the whales.

Hanover, January 22, 1959

When I returned to New London I learned that while I had been talking about the Arctic, the Navy Department had been doing something about it. The *Skate* was scheduled to return to the Polar Sea in March and investigate the possibility of wintertime operations.

Could we really break our way through the ice to reach the surface? If so, the sail of the *Skate* would have to act as our battering ram as we rose vertically upward out of the depths. This sail is filled with nearly a dozen hydraulically hoisted masts, antennas, periscopes, and ventilation pipes. Most of these devices are vital to the safe operation of the submarine. Could they stand the splintering shock as the three-thousand-ton ship drove them into the ice?

Several of these masts run up and down in long, watertight tubes that penetrate into the interior of the *Skate*. If the sail were damaged, one of these tubes could be twisted off to become a knife in the back of the ship.

The sail structure, which had been strengthened for the summer expedition in the event the ship should inadvertently strike the ice, was now to be further altered and protected for the task that lay ahead. Powerful floodlights would be installed in the deck to illuminate the ice from underneath in the winter darkness. A special closed-circuit television system would be installed to help us examine it. The camera would be imbedded in the deck in a watertight container and so mounted that it could be trained in various directions by remote control.

In my mind's eye I could see the *Skate*, groping silently in the dark, searching with floodlights and television for a place to break through the ice. Had our good judgment been carried away by the successes of one ten-day period in the most favorable season of the year?

My doubts notwithstanding, workmen swarmed over the *Skate* from one end to the other, installing new equipment. An improved type of topside fathometer was being put in under the personal supervision of Waldo Lyon, and the famous scientist himself was going along on this trip. The man who had been going to the Arctic in submarines since 1947 wanted to witness this new step in exploration of the northern sea for himself.

One day, while all this work was going on, a phone call summoned me to the office of Admiral Warder. He greeted me with his customary geniality, and told me he had a proposal for me.

"Jim," he said, "you thought a lot of Sir Hubert Wilkins, didn't you?"

I nodded.

"How would you like to do a last favor for him?" he said.

I was taken aback. "I don't understand," I said.

The Admiral told me that he had received a telephone call from some friends of Wilkins in New York. Between the time Sir Hubert had visited the *Skate* and the time of his death he had expressed to Lady Wilkins the hope that when he died his ashes might someday be carried to the North Pole by submarine and there distributed. The man who was perhaps best remembered as an arctic flyer, and whose career had in one way or another been continually involved with aviation, had nonetheless asked that his last trip be made under the polar ice. His heart still belonged to the *Nautilus*. It had been his supreme effort of daring imagination. The partial failure of the expedition had never dampened his enthusiasm for the dream that lay behind it.

"The *Skate* would be honored, Admiral," I said. "But to surface right at the Pole is a pretty big order. We couldn't do it last August, and I don't hold much hope for the winter."

The Admiral suggested that we might perform the task while submerged, using a special ejector—possibly a torpedo tube.

I shook my head vigorously. "No there's no meaning to that. He wouldn't have wanted it that way."

The Admiral agreed. "You're right—either do it on the surface, or bring the ashes back and we'll have somebody do it at a more favorable time."

This ended the conversation, but not my thoughts about it. Somehow, I felt, we would have to find a way.

CHAPTER 3

Sailing day was set for the third of March. As the time approached, our organization was shuffled to be ready for the task that lay ahead. In December, John Nicholson had been ordered to his own command; Bill Layman moved up to take his place. Big, cheerful, redheaded Guy Shaffer replaced Bill Cowhill as diving officer to allow for the changes necessary to make Dave Boyd the new chief engineer.

There was no question that the transfer of Nicholson was a severe loss, but aside from this one change, the crew that would take the *Skate* to the winter Arctic remained essentially the same as the one that had piloted her under the polar ice in August. For this I was thankful. We would need all the confidence and team spirit that we could muster.

In the meantime, the civilian specialists and scientists began to gather. Old shipmate Zane Sandusky reappeared to make the necessary tests of the inertial navigator. This time his assistant was Bob Wadell, the genial Schmidt being tied up in other work. We were all glad to hear that Zane was going with us, even though we had not completely forgiven him for complaining about the food in Paris during a brief visit following our cruise last September. With everyone else exchanging enthusiastic recommendations on fine restaurants, the unreconstructed American Sandusky hovered dolefully on the edge of starvation until he found a place where he could get good hamburgers and fried potatoes. *Sacre bleu!*

Hard at work on our television installation was Cramer Bacque, a rotund, jolly, and highly competent young engineer from the Bendix Corporation. Cramer, however, was having his troubles. No one had ever put a movable television camera into a submarine before, and it was providing quite a problem. The camera had to be encased in a huge watertight steel container with a thick glass window. This container then had to be mounted so that it could be trained from within the ship in almost every direction. Cramer had his hands full, not only with the technical difficulties involved but also with the problem of completing the job by the third of March.

Several times during the fall Dave Boyd had spoken wistfully of his conversation with the skindivers at Station Alfa. David thought we ought to have equipment along so that we could examine pressure ridges at first hand from underneath, in the hope of unraveling some of the mysteries of their formation. Dr. Arnest was also a skindiving enthusiast, and, through their repeated urgings, it was finally arranged for Boyd, Arnest, the doctor's assistant Richard Brown, and soundman Sam Hall to go to diving school in Washington for formal instruction. Fortunately, the Navy does not allow its men simply to put on aqualungs and take off for the bottom—not while they are on duty, anyway.

These four men underwent a rigorous two-week training period. They were given special exercises to strengthen important muscles—and were told to keep them up when they got back to the *Skate*. They were taught how to disassemble and repair the aqualung; they were taught what to do if they lost the mouthpiece under water; they were taught what to do if their facemasks came off or flooded. The head of the school knew these men might be swimming in very cold water (but he did not know where) and saw to it that they obtained the right equipment for it.

The four returned with quarter-inch-thick black sponge-rubber suits which completely covered them all but their faces. When they went into the icy depths, the sponge rubber would absorb and hold water which would become warm from body contact and would act as an insulator against the debilitating chill of the sea. It was hoped that the divers could stay in near-freezing water for up to half an hour with no ill effects.

Dave and the doctor were full of enthusiasm when they returned from Washington, but I was by no means sure I wanted them to go under the ice. I must admit that I had no desire to go myself. Of course, in the event of damage to the ship, the ability to get into the water for examination and repairs might prove invaluable. It was probably this consideration which impelled the Navy Department to give our men the aqualung training.

A few days before our departure, another former shipmate rejoined us—Walt Wittmann. Walt had spent much of his time digging up information on the arctic winter and came armed with a mountain of literature. There was enough to keep us reading all the way to the North Pole.

Finally we were finished. The television system was installed —we could stand in the control center of the *Skate* and examine our surroundings at the Electric Boat dock by remote control as the giant steel barrel holding the camera swiveled in its mounting. Tilting it back, we could see plainly the top of the sail, with the periscopes and antennas sticking from it like toothpicks. Dr. Lyon's new ice fathometer was put in. Zane Sandusky and Bob Wadell said the inertial navigator was in tip-top shape. Our sail structure had been modified for better protection. The floodlights which had been built into the deck and the sail seemed bright enough to illuminate the whole arctic basin. What the wealth of our country could do for us, it had done; the rest was up to us.

All that remained were the good-bys. Nancy and I have been married for seventeen years, but the partings seem harder each time. The week or two before are spoiled because of the unmentioned but ever-present knowledge that "the day" isn't far away. The last days are only made bearable for husband and wife in the solace which the perspective of experience brings. Time does pass, and returns are sweet.

But not so for the children. Good-by for them is good-by. In their brave young way they don't talk much about it, but it's a burden they find hard to bear.

It was three-year-old Charlie who nearly broke my heart. When all the farewells were said he came toddling out to the car nodding his head.

His trusting face looked up at me: "You won't be gone so long *this* time, will you Daddy?" he entreated. "Back *soooon?*"

And then Nancy, standing behind him, could no longer keep back the tears.

It was a cold, still, dark day. The Electric Boat docks were momentarily quiet as the workmen turned to watch. Al Kelln and I were on the bridge, looking down on the pier beside us. Only one manila line remained between it and the bow of the submarine.

"Take in number one," Al shouted through cupped hands. "All back two-thirds," he said more quietly into the intercom which carried his words down to the control center. Silently the ship trembled with the surge of power and the surface swirled astern. The black hull of the *Skate* swung out into the Thames. The propellers were reversed and we headed out into Block Island Sound and the open sea. The familiar shoreline faded into a blurred line, so that I could barely see the white houses of Mystic when I looked back with the glasses. Soon the bow started to rise and fall with the slow rhythm of the Atlantic swell.

For the second time in seven months, the *Skate* was bound to the North Pole and beyond. I remained on the bridge until we reached water deep enough for diving. Then I went down the ladder and into the control center. A few moments later Al sounded the diving alarm from the bridge and followed, securing the hatch behind him and dogging it shut as he came.

The bow knifed into the gray waters of the March Atlantic and down we glided, below the troubled waters at the surface and into the quiet deep. We set our course for Nantucket Shoals —and for Prins Karls Forland, 4000 miles beyond.

CHAPTER 4

As the *Skate* sped northward her crew handled her with veteran skill and confidence. The smooth routine was broken occasionally when navigator Layman brought the ship to periscope depth to shoot the sun. Only at these times were we in contact with the storm-tossed swells of the wintry North Atlantic. As we approached the surface, giant seas began to toss the ship about almost as though she were riding the wavecrests. The periscope would be clear one minute, submerged under tons of cascading green water the next. The winter gales tore the tops from the waves and sent them scudding across the water in streaks of gray foam. It was with a real sense of relief that we heard Layman say he was finished with his sights and we could drop back to the deep, quiet waters below and proceed on our way unconcerned with the storm above.

Inside the ship, the usual good-natured banter of men at sea went on. Lieutenant Dick Boyle, a bachelor who was new on board, was the proud possessor of a very expensive Mercedes-Benz sports car. All of us kidded Dick about his flashy extravagance, while he protested earnestly that this was really a utilitarian car used by conservative, hard-working businessmen in Europe. It didn't take us long to find a magazine ad with an exact duplicate of Dick's car pictured at the top of a San Francisco hill. Inside was a glamorous-looking couple, dressed to the nines and obviously on pleasure bent, the girl gaily waving a bottle of vermouth. We gleefully tore it out and presented it to Dick, inscribed "Just plain working folks."

In the crew's mess, the veterans of the summer before made preparations to initiate the few new hands on board as we crossed the Arctic Circle. When the day arrived, elaborate ceremonies were held; the neophytes were brought before a judge, who was dressed gaudily in red-dyed long underwear. Each victim, blind-folded, was required to sit in a puddle of ice water, completing an electrical circuit that gave him a mild jolt. Of course all the neophytes were kept locked in another room so that they had no idea what to expect. Each succeeding prisoner produced the same reaction of surprise, and each brought roars of laughter from the veterans.

The judge finally sentenced the neophyte to have his nose painted blue with dye and be fitted with absurd snow goggles with which he was forced to grope his way about the ship.

The Arctic Circle is far south of the polar ice pack, and we still had many miles to go before we would find ice. Meanwhile, we were all becoming more and more impressed by the learned Dr. Lyon, who took our arctic education in hand during the cruise north. Slight, soft-spoken, and unobtrusive, he had a manner that fitted well the necessary atmosphere on board a submarine. Not the sort whose strong personality makes an immediate impression, it was nevertheless not long before his quiet self-assurance and keen mind gained him rapt and respectful attention.

One afternoon as we neared Spitsbergen he gave a fascinating talk in the wardroom on a subject that was strange to us: has the Arctic Ocean always been covered with ice?

He asked us to assume, for the sake of discussion, that the Arctic Ocean was ice-free. What difference would this make to the world? A great deal. Instead of a five-million-square-mile desert at the top of the world, there would be a live, stormy ocean. Gone would be the icy waste which acts as an insulation and reflector to the rays of the sun, limiting the amount of moisture evaporated from the surface. Instead, the open water of the Arctic would pour moisture into the earth's atmosphere, to be precipitated in the form of rain and snow and hail, much of which would fall on the northern land masses—Greenland, Canada, Alaska, Siberia, and northern Europe. As the years went by these layers of ice and snow would build up and up and up, and huge glaciers would be formed from the rich water supply. When these inevitably could no longer be contained in the far north, like the leviathan rivers of ice they are, they would press their way southward. Over Norway into Europe; over Canada into the United States; over Siberia into the heart of Russia. Another ice age would have arrived.

This, said Lyon, was possibly what caused the mysterious advance of the previous ice ages, the last one twelve thousand or so years ago.

What caused them finally to retreat? As long as we were building theories, Dr. Lyon said, we might as well go on. The amount of moisture trapped in such glaciers would be enormous. Enough to cause the levels of the world's oceans to lower significantly. And this would have a considerable effect on the Arctic Ocean. The warm waters of the Gulf Stream push up into the Norwegian Sea along the coast of Norway and creep along the northern coast of Russia, finally blending with the Arctic Ocean. (It was this warm current that Nansen followed when he sailed the *Fram* eastward to lodge her in the ice.) To get into the polar basin the Gulf Stream must pass through relatively shallow water north of Norway. Now, if the level of the Atlantic dropped far enough, the access of the warming Gulf Stream to the Arctic would be cut off. And then the Arctic Ocean would freeze once more.

With the Arctic once more a frozen desert, the glaciers would be starved for moisture and would slowly start to retreat. The ice age would be ended. Eventually enough of the moisture from the melting glaciers would find its way back into the other oceans of the world so that their levels would begin to rise once more. The Gulf Stream would again be able to force its way into the Arctic Ocean. The cycle could start again.

Is this the part of the cycle we are now in—a slowly warming Arctic which will gradually lose its white cover and become an open ocean? No one knows for sure.

It was Saturday afternoon, the fourteenth of March. I felt the deck incline upward under my feet as we swung the *Skate* toward the surface. The periscope broke the water in a choppy sea and peered out into murky weather. It was almost dark, although it was only two o'clock. Navigation showed us to be just off Prins Karls Forland, but I could see no land.

"Raise the radar mast," I called out. Hydraulic oil hissed as the mast rose. Soon the pulses of our radar were sweeping the barren coast that our eyes could not see.

"There she is!" called Bill Layman. "Right where she ought to be!" I lowered the periscope and walked aft. There was our island unmistakably outlined on the glass tube like an illuminated string bean.

I thought back to a Saturday afternoon seven months earlier when we had been at this same spot doing the same thing. And I thought of another August afternoon twenty-seven years earlier, when another submarine had gone by Prins Karls on her way to the ice pack. She had plodded by on the surface, with one balky diesel engine clanking away, the other one shut down for repairs, and her crew clamoring to turn back before it was too late. But within her had been a man with a stubborn will that bent the others to his wishes. They had kept on going north.

Now all that remained on earth of that iron will and great spirit was in my room in a small bronze urn. Sir Hubert was passing Prins Karls once more.

CHAPTER 5

Once we had obtained our position by radar we dove to 400 feet and set our course northward. Within a few hours Dr. Lyon's new ice detector began to sketch sudden dips from the smooth line of open water. The ice pack—its boundaries much farther south than last summer—was upon us. Dr. Lyon bent anxiously over the new machine, making careful adjustments which brought the ice profiles into sharp focus as we passed under the thin cover of block and brash.

The ice machine, however, was no longer the main attraction for the curious crew. Instead, a large group was clustered about the television screen with as much fascination as if it had been showing the first game of the World Series. Even with the poor illumination of the arctic twilight, shadowy images of the huge ice blocks drifting overhead were outlined plainly. The instrument barrier had been broken—at last we could see!

The fact remained, though, that we were heading back underneath the ice, and, as on our cruise last summer, this had an immediate impact on all of us. By nine in the evening the ice had closed solidly overhead; the television screen showed nothing but solid black. One by one, the men gathered around it wandered away without saying anything.

We were running along smoothly when, about midnight, Dave Boyd called me to say there was trouble in the engine room. The seal around one of the propeller shafts was leaking. I went hastily to the engine room, where I found Dave crouched worriedly in the crowded corner aft. As he shone his flashlight into the dark corner I could see a steady jet of water streaming out around the bottom of the spinning shaft where it penetrated the hull. The sea was coming in.

Water was collecting in the engine-room bilges. It was still not rising very fast—our pumps could easily keep up with it—but it easily might get worse. For a moment, I thought of turning back before we got any farther under the ice.

"What do you think?" I asked Dave.

"Well, we can try backing the shaft," he replied. "Sometimes that seats the seal."

I nodded in agreement. "Starboard back two-thirds!" I shouted above the roar of machinery. The shaft hissed to a quick stop, then began spinning swiftly in the opposite direction. As the huge propeller bit into the water the submarine shuddered and shook from one end to the other.

Suddenly we recoiled from a shower of icy salt spray which exploded from the seal in all directions. The air seemed filled with flying water. What had gone wrong? The ship continued to shudder and shake as the great propeller chewed the water just outside the hull, and the noise was deafening.

Then—as suddenly as one turns off a faucet—the water stopped. "Stop the shaft!" I shouted. The shuddering ceased; all was quiet. Only a trickle of water came from the seal.

I was limp with relief. "Wow!" I exclaimed weakly.

"We've still got to be careful," Dave said. "When that seal shifts it sometimes jams, and then you're in real trouble. Ready to try her ahead?"

I nodded, and called out the order to the maneuvering room. Once more the throttles were opened, and steam hissed into the turbines. Slowly the shaft started to turn, spinning faster and faster as the *Skate* slowly regained speed. Finally we reached 16 knots. The seal held.

Still deeply disturbed, I walked slowly forward through the reactor compartment to my room. Everything had gone so well on the first cruise under the ice—almost too well. And now we were going back under circumstances when everything had to work absolutely perfectly. We couldn't stand many incidents like this. Was our luck about to turn against us?

That night, for once, I could not sleep.

Before breakfast next morning I walked into the control center to have a look at the ice detector. Walt Wittmann stood by the machine writing busily.

"How's it look, Walt?" I asked.

"This is something," Walt said, shaking his head. "Not one bit of open water during the night. Over a hundred and ninety miles and nothing but ice."

I whistled in amazement. "I thought for sure we'd find a little open water this far south even in March."

Walt shrugged. "There've been some thin spots here and there," he said, "but not a trace of open water."

I walked over to the television screen. It was getting light above and the ice was once more visible. However, here was quite a different picture from that of the drifting blocks of yesterday. Now huge black patches of floe ice could be seen, outlined in the dim light which filtered through the thinner ice surrounding them. It was rather like looking up through a gigantic fruit jello salad. There was no sign of a break in this translucent ceiling.

We were now extremely anxious to make a practice surfacing in open water before we got too far north to find any. Guy Shaffer had never even had an opportunity to attempt the delicate maneuver of slowly raising the ship from a dead halt; the sea had been so rough on our way north that it would have been pointless to try it there.

Almost as an echo to my thoughts came a report from Pat Garner, who was officer of the deck, that he was turning around to investigate possible open water. Possible open water—that sounded strange. Last summer it either was or it wasn't.

When I went to look at the trace on the ice machine I saw what had everyone confused. Hour after hour the stylus had been tracing an unbroken ceiling of heavy ice—mile after mile of thick floes with an occasional pressure-ridge stalactite. Now the stylus had jumped up and was drawing out a long flat line. But there was a faint hint of fuzziness—the line was not clean and sharp as last summer's open-water traces had been. Was our new ice machine faulty, or was this the sign of thin ice?

We circled back and stopped under the suspected opening. The television showed nothing but murky gray. The periscope was not much more help. I could make out only a faint aquamarine light coming through from above. It didn't look like open water but I had to keep in mind that even at 9 in the morning the sun was barely over the horizon. It would be like early dawn up there.

I told Guy to raise the ship to 100 feet, where we could examine the situation closely. He carefully pumped out ballast water and up we drifted. I looked in vain for the heavy blocks and jagged edges which had been so familiar a part of the polynya icescape. There was only a faint greenish-blue glow from above as far as the eye could see.

"I think we're under a large lead that has frozen over," I announced. "Don't believe the ice is too heavy—I can see some light coming through from above." I turned to Al Kelln at the ice detector. "How thick do you think it is?"

"Can't tell for sure," he replied. "This scale is just not small enough."

"Can you make a guess?" I asked.

"Well, it has to be less than three feet," he said, "but it could be as thin as four or five inches."

I had hoped to avoid this eventuality, searching instead for open water in which we might quickly rehearse last summer's proven methods. But here was an opportunity too attractive to miss.

It was Sunday morning. It had also been a Sunday morning last August when we took our first big step—and a mighty successful one it had proved to be. As long as men go to sea, I suppose, a thread of superstition will run through the things they do and the decisions they make. No matter how modern the ship, old traditions and beliefs of the sea hang on. The forces to be dealt with are too vast, the vicissitudes of fate too capricious, for men to deal with the sea only with cold logic.

My mind was made up. "Stand by to hit the ice!" I called out. "Bring her up," I told Guy.

The whir of the trimming pump filled the room as the *Skate* slowly began to rise out of the dark depths.

"Snap on the floodlights," I ordered. "Up periscope." I was disappointed to see that the lights were of little help. It was like turning on car headlights in a fog. We were bathed in a heavy yellow mist. However, even in the hazy glare I could see our familiar friends of last summer, the jellyfish. Their delicate rainbow-hued tentacles waved languidly as we drifted by them. Wherever the ocean is—even here, in its darkest, coldest corner —there is life.

I finally turned off the floodlights. We were now so close to the ice that the periscope had to come down for safety. Now I could see nothing. We trained the Cyclops eye of the television around in the hope that it would help. Nothing.

We decided to train the television camera on the part of the ship which would take the initial shock—the sail.

"Turn on the sail floodlight," I ordered. A ghostly cone of light appeared on the upper part of the screen. Far above we could see a faint disk where the floodlight illuminated the ice. The cone of light became smaller and brighter as we rose. Everyone instinctively braced himself for the shock.

Suddenly there was a sensation like that of being on an elevator stopped too quickly. My stomach turned over. There was no noise of collision, and no further feeling of motion. But on the television screen, the disk of light on the ice was getting larger, the cone growing longer—we were dropping away!

I glanced at the depth gauge. We had passed 100 feet and were still falling. Desperately, Guy Shaffer pumped out water to regain our stability. Blowing the ballast tanks would have been faster, but with ice overhead it was unthinkable. We had to rely on the slower pumps.

Guy had checked our downward motion at 150 feet. By television we examined the sail for damage. None was apparent.

"We'll hit it again," I said with determination. "Harder this time." Again we started up. Again the whir of the trimming pump announced our progress. Again the cone of light narrowed as we neared the ice. Holding my breath, I braced my back against the periscope stand, watching the television screen as though hypnotized.

Again a sickening lurch as we hit—but now the television screen was filled with the image of splashing water and bits of shattered ice. A heavy grinding crunch shook the control center. The top of the sail disappeared from the screen. We were through!

"Up periscope."

I gripped the handles and put my face against the eyepiece. It was as though I were looking into a freshly laundered pillowcase. Nothing but dead white. I shifted the prism of the optics in the hope they would clear. Nothing.

Then I understood what had happened. As soon as the wet periscope had reached the frigid arctic air, a film of ice had formed on its lens. I folded up the handles of the useless scope and looked at the depth gauge. We had come to rest at about 42 feet—just about the same as last summer. I assumed that we were floating with our sail out of the ice and the rest of the ship under water. The television camera, embedded in the main deck was still submerged and could help us no more.

I hesitated a moment. What to do? Blowing the tanks to bring the ship up the rest of the way might be dangerous, especially if the delicate rudder were under heavy ice. But there was really no choice. We had to take the chance. We would not have any clear idea of our surroundings until I could reach the bridge.

"Blow the main ballast, Guy," I said. "But take it very easy."

The valves sending air to the main ballast tanks were cautiously opened, and the hiss and chatter of high-pressure air filled the room. Nothing happened for a few moments, then the *Skate* again started to move slowly upward. We listened carefully for the sound of breaking ice or crunching metal, but could hear nothing over the noise of the air.

Finally the *Skate* was high enough that I knew the hatch leading to the bridge was above the water. The ship was still well below normal surface draft but appeared to be holding her trim satisfactorily. I told Shaffer to stop blowing the tanks.

Quartermaster John Medaglia climbed the ladder leading through the tube to the hatch.

"Open the hatch!" I shouted to him. My ears felt the slight change in air pressure as the heavy metal hatch swung back and banged against its stop. Medaglia went up as soon as he opened it. Ordinarily he crosses the platform at this level and climbs a second ladder to the bridge, but I found him standing on the platform, arms akimbo, looking at the small ladder opening. It was jammed with huge pieces of ice!

I shouted down to the control center for a man with a heavy crowbar. This was probably the last thing they expected me to ask for, but in only a few minutes husky fireman Roger Schlief was chopping away at the obstruction.

The small enclosure resounded with the fragments of ice tumbling down around us. At last it was clear enough for me to get to the bridge.

I went up the ladder, squeezed past several ice blocks, then climbed on top of one for a better view.

The pale blue melt ponds and black patches of open water of last summer were gone and in their place was a world of stark whiteness. The black sail of the *Skate* was poking up through the center of an enormous flat plain—a frozen lead so large that I could see only that it wandered to the horizon. There was no wind but the air was biting cold.

Setting off the white of the snow-covered ice was a beautifully soft sky of rose and lavender to the southeast, where the morning sun peeped above the rim of our frozen world. At this season, I knew, it would not rise far above the horizon, and the day would be one of perpetual twilight. There was no sign of life, and the stillness of the air seemed in keeping with the beauty of the scene.

Medaglia joined me on the bridge and this glib young man was speechless. Neither of us spoke; we knew that nothing we could say could express the wonder of what we felt.

Finally I leaned over to talk to the control center on the intercom, but found that it was frozen and useless. The *Skate* was still in a perilous situation, balanced just at the surface, and she might suddenly start to sink. The sail was noticeably low —Medaglia and I were only 10 feet or so above the ice. It was essential to establish close communications with the control center.

Medaglia went below to explain the situation, and an emergency telephone circuit was quickly rigged. By this means I ordered Guy Shaffer to go ahead with the blowing of the tanks.

The *Skate* gradually began to press against the underside of the ice along her entire length. Faint bulges appeared in the ice. Then, although air continued to pour into the tanks, nothing more happened: the ship stopped rising. Perhaps this was the place to halt, I thought; we could just leave her like this. But no—we had come up here to find out if we could surface, and surface we would.

Then, without warning, the *Skate* began to break through the ice like an enormous cookie-cutter. Up she came, staggering under the heavy load of ice that remained on her deck. Aft, the rudder punched a neat hole for itself; protruding from the ice it looked like the fin of a gigantic shark.

There was no open water visible at the edge of the ship. She was held securely in the confining ice—no need to worry about drifting. We would stay where we were.

Bill Layman joined me on the bridge and, after a moment of awed silence, suggested that he take my place while I put on something warmer. Only then did I realize that in my excitement I had come up on the bridge with nothing heavier than a parka and that I was getting colder every minute.

Medaglia was measuring the temperature as I went below. It was 20 degrees below zero.

Before long I was encased in the stout clothes that had been issued to us especially for the cruise, bulky trousers and a jacket of olive-drab nylon quilted over foam rubber and a helmetlike head covering. I then returned to the bridge, anxious to examine the ship to see if we had been damaged breaking through the ice.

Several men were busy with crowbars removing the ice blocks from the deck. It was a simple matter to slide down the sloping side of *Skate*'s superstructure and onto the ice surrounding the ship. I immediately walked back to examine the rudder, which stuck up through the ice some 15 feet aft of the rest of the ship. It did not appear to have suffered any damage, nor did the rest of the ship. The whalebacked sail had taken the original impact without harm, and then it had been a matter of slowly and carefully pushing the rest of the ship up to enlarge the hole started by the sail.

Elated, I walked farther away from the ship to gain some perspective of her position. (After all, not many skippers have the opportunity, this far from land, to stroll out and take a look at their ships from a distance.) Her black hull looked as though it had been dropped gently on the smooth surface of the ice like a confectioner's decoration on a white cake frosting. It seemed inconceivable that she could ever move again.

Even in my special gear, I soon began to feel the cold and decided to return. Getting back up the sloping sides of the ship was not as easy as getting down, but a piece of line had been rigged and I pulled myself up with it. Getting ready to go out on the ice was Lieutenant Bruce Meader, our official photographer. Bruce, a naturally husky young man, looked like a well-stuffed teddy bear in his heavy arctic clothes. He had cameras slung over both shoulders and was trying to slide carefully down the side of the ship without damaging anything.

"Better get a lot of pictures, Bruce," I told him. "No one'll believe this unless you do!"

"I see what you mean," he said, looking at our surroundings with the same wonder the rest of us had felt.

Later, when Bruce brought his chilled cameras back inside the warm ship, moisture from the air condensed and froze on them. In minutes his elegant Leicas and Nikons were encrusted in white rime like the coils of an old-fashioned refrigerator.

During lunch, Dr. Lyon suggested wistfully that he would very much like to get motion pictures of the *Skate* actually breaking through the ice so that he could study the exact manner in which the breaking occurred. We all laughed. Someone said it would be like getting pictures of the first landing on the moon.

After lunch, however, while I stood on the bridge talking to Guy Shaffer and looking around at the wide expanse of the frozen lead, I thought about Dr. Lyon's suggestion. What better chance to do just what he wanted? We could leave Bruce Meader out on the ice, submerge, move a few yards forward, and surface again.

"How about it, Guy?" I asked. "Think we could do it?"

"Sure," he chuckled, "if Bruce will agree to getting out there on that ice alone. I'm not sure *I'd* want to!"

I decided it might be better to send some company with Bruce. It also occurred to me that it would be wise to get them going before they had too much time to think about it. I told Chief Dornberg to organize a party consisting of himself, Dr. Arnest, Bruce Meader, and a quartermaster to go out on the ice and take some pictures of the ship.

I didn't say under what circumstances, but the word got around pretty fast. Dave Boyd and Pat Garner supplied Bruce with a box of emergency rations, a Boy Scout compass, and a waterproof chart of the area. They told him soberly that, while we would make every effort to retrieve him, he ought to realize we might not be able to make it. They advised him that if we didn't come up in two hours, he'd better start walking south.

Bruce didn't view this expedition as lightly as his mischievous shipmates, who, he pointed out, were going to remain safe inside the ship.

The photographing party assembled on the bridge, and I gave them brief instructions. One member, quartermaster Alex Martin, came puffing up the ladder at the last minute, missing some of my explanation. I figured the others would fill him in.

As soon as the party was clear of the ship, Guy and I went below and started to submerge. The vents of the main ballast tanks cracked open in the icy stillness and the *Skate* began to settle in the water. The periscope had been cleaned of its film of ice and I could see reasonably well. There were billows of steam at both ends of the ship as the warm air from the tanks struck the frigid air.

Through the periscope it looked as though the *Skate* were slowly sinking into the ground. Then the periscope went under. On the television screen we could see a long cigar-shaped hole in the ice above us. It was a perfect outline of the *Skate*.

The sight of this hole on the television screen gave us a simple landmark. Using it as a reference point we could tell how far away we had moved. We eased steam into the turbines and let the *Skate* move barely ahead, then reversed the propellers and stopped her.

When our friends the jellyfish told us that we had come to a complete halt, we started upward. This time we came through nicely. One of the crew immediately went up to clear the ice we knew would block the hatch and soon I was on the bridge waving to the forlorn-looking party on the ice. I could see that they had been in perfect position to take pictures.

"Get some good ones?" I shouted hopefully.

No reply. It was obvious something had gone wrong.

At last Meader called out, "My camera froze. I didn't get a thing."

The four men were pretty subdued as they trooped in off the ice. Alex Martin looked especially crestfallen.

"That deal was sure cooked up in a hurry," he complained. "I had no idea what was going on until I saw the ship start to go down! Next time I go on one of these ice picnics I'd like to know more about it!"

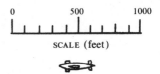

```
0          500        1000
├─┴─┴─┴─┴─┼─┴─┴─┴─┴─┤
        SCALE (feet)
```

The ice pack in mid-March, photographed from a height of 18,000 feet.
The arctic dawn casts long shadows across pressure ridges on the
ice. A typical winter lead meanders between two floes, its surface
already covered with young ice. The sketch of the submarine at
lower right shows the comparative size of the *Skate*.

James F. Calvert / National Geographic Image Collection

Dave Boyd and Dick Boyle affix the flag
in an ice cairn at the North Pole.

Pressure ridges often tower far taller than the height of a man.

The rudder punches a neat hole for itself as the submarine surfaces through the winter ice.

At the North Pole, by the lurid light of red flares, the author reads a memorial service for Sir **Hubert** Wilkins.

Al Kelln clings to the radio mast while repairing
a damaged antenna in 23-below cold.

The *Skate* surfaced in a narrow lead
which stretches to the horizon.

The *Skate* on the table-smooth surface
of a large frozen lead.

The winter sun hangs low above the horizon as two crewmen strike out over the moonlike landscape of a frozen lead.

Dr. Arnest and Dave Boyd in
heavy insulating sponge-rubber
suits prepare to dive beneath the ice.

From the periscope stand in the control center,
the author gives orders to surface.

CHAPTER 6

About five in the afternoon we submerged and set our course for the North Pole. All through the night as we sped northward the ice detector and television scanned the surface in vain for patches of thin ice. It began to seem that our belief we would find thin ice frequently enough to surface at will was overly optimistic. Our plan to surface precisely at the North Pole began to look hopeless.

Cramer Bacque had a daily routine for checking out his television set to make sure it was operating properly. Part of this process involved switching on the forward floodlight and using the beam of light it threw as a sort of test pattern while he adjusted and focused his camera. On Monday, Cramer was working away at this task. The upward cone of light was plainly visible in the television screen and it became alternately sharp and fuzzy as Cramer adjusted the controls.

Suddenly the screen was flooded with fish. At first we thought Cramer's adjustments had gone awry, making things appear on the screen which didn't belong there. But as he adjusted the focus the fish appeared even more clearly.

Individually they were fairly small—no more than 8 inches long—but their numbers seemed countless. Men came from all over the ship to watch the show. Here we were, 400 feet below the surface and less than 300 miles from the North Pole—what sort of fish could they be? No one could be sure, but both Dr. Lyon and Walt Wittmann thought they most closely resembled ordinary North Atlantic herring. The school was enormous. On we went, mile after mile, and the sea appeared full of fish. It was possible that the same school of fish remained with us, attracted by the light, but we were speeding along at 16 knots, a fairly stiff pace for such little fellows to keep up. Furthermore, they didn't appear to be swimming along with us; rather, we seemed to be passing through them.

The hypnotically undulating pattern was rudely broken when a huge black shape shot suddenly through the picture, jaws agape and eye flashing. And that's about all the description I can give. All of us were watching closely at the time but whatever it was came and went too swiftly for identification. It was apparent that he was up to no good, and at first we all thought it was some sort of predatory fish. Afterward it occurred to us that it might also have been a seal, but whether or not seals can go that deep is not known.

The appearance of the stranger did not spoil the show, however. As we sped on, the lithe shapes of the school continued to flit through our floodlight. The black villain never returned. Then, as suddenly as they had appeared, the fish were gone. Who knows how many other displays of nature we missed beneath the arctic ice simply for lack of eyes to see them?

Late that afternoon our ice machine again showed the peculiar trace that indicated thin ice. How thin we had no way of telling, but it looked worth a try. When we plotted its outline, it was plain that this lead was not as large as Sunday's but was large enough to use if the ice could be broken.

As we hovered under it, motionless, I could see the dim green-blue glow of the thin ice enclosed in the inky black of the surrounding floes. It was apparent that the amount of light we could see coming through the ice would be an important factor in determining whether or not the ice was thin enough to break. If the ice looked black, or even dark, from underneath, getting through it was probably out of the question.

This brought up the question of how much light was above the ice to start with. That would depend on where the sun was (which we could calculate from the *Nautical Almanac*) and the amount of overcast (which we had absolutely no way of knowing). It promised to be a guessing game.

As we rose slowly toward the ice, I suddenly noticed the ice was moving in relation to the *Skate*. As I watched through the periscope, the jellyfish around us remained stationary but the ominous shadows of the heavy ice were moving slowly but surely. Either the ice was moving, or a current was moving us. This made surfacing the ship in the desired spot far more difficult.

The periscope had to be lowered, and the television was trained on the top of the sail. It was darker this time, and the beam of the floodlight shone more brightly than before. We hit the ice with the same stomach-lifting bump we had felt the day before. The television screen showed the ice shattering and the sail passing through it. Then, for no apparent reason, we started to sink. Whether it was the effect of the impact or some change in buoyancy, we didn't know, but down we went.

Worse than that, the television showed the neat hole we had punched in the ice was drifting away; we were faced with the prospect of breaking a new one. Undismayed, Guy Shaffer commenced pumping out more water to send us on our way up again. I noticed that the continued sidewise drift of the ice was bringing us closer and closer to the edge of the lead, where the ice would be too heavy to break, and where there was a grave risk of damaging the ship. I wanted Guy to bring her up faster, but realized that hitting the ice at too high a speed could be fatal. If we should hit the ice hard and it turned out to be too thick to break. . . . Well, there was no use telling Guy to hurry.

Finally we were at the point of impact. The control center grew tense in anticipation. *Crunch!* We were through, and this time we held our position.

Again we gently blew the ballast tanks to bring the upper hatch out of the water. When Medaglia and I reached the passageway to the bridge, it was jammed with ice even heavier than that of the day before. However, the crowbars went speedily to work and soon I was on the bridge again.

This time the scene was quite different. We were only four degrees of latitude from the North Pole, the sun was slightly below the horizon, and the sky was heavily overcast. The *Skate* was surfaced in a frozen lead whose sides were marked by heavy hummocks of pressure ice—the black shadows I had seen through the periscope. The ice on the lead was covered with perhaps half an inch of snow and looked as smooth as a table-top. Beyond the pressure ridges the icefields stretched unbroken to the horizon. They were covered with the scalloped form of snow called *sastrugi,* whose wind-eroded curls looked as if they had been sculptured in crisp meringue.

The brooding sky hung heavily over the white waste; gone was the fragile beauty of yesterday's scene and in its place was an atmosphere of depression and foreboding. The wind was very light. No life could be seen.

The place where we had first broken through the ice and then fallen away was about 50 yards to starboard, a ragged cobalt puddle in the snow-covered ice.

Glancing aft at the top of the sail I saw that one of the radio antennas had been damaged. Built to telescope within itself for protection, the internal part had been bent when a small piece of ice jammed down into it. I called Al Kelln to come up and have a look at it.

He clambered aft over the slippery whaleback and examined the antenna closely, then returned to the bridge.

"We'll never be able to use that antenna again until that center part is renewed," he said grimly.

"How much trouble will it be?" I asked.

"Plenty, I'm afraid. The mast'll have to be all the way up when we thread in the new piece."

"We need that antenna, Al," I said. "You know the flap it'll cause if we don't get some word off on how we're getting along."

Al nodded agreement. "There's only one way to do it. We'll have to strap someone to the mast and let him ride it up as we raise it."

Fully raised, the antenna mast was over 10 feet higher than the sail and anyone swinging from the top of the mast would be nearly 35 feet above the ice.

Al stared up at the damaged mast. "I'll do it myself, Captain," he said. "That's the best way."

In a few minutes one of Al's radiomen lashed him to the mast with manila line.

"Ready to go. Raise the mast," said Kelln. The faint hiss of hydraulic oil could be heard as the mast crept slowly upward in the frigid air. Kelln made a strange picture, silhouetted against the lowering gray sky.

Occasionally, when he needed another tool or a spare part, we would lower the mast, give him what he needed, and send him up again. He found that he could not work with his gloves on, and I worried about his hands in the 20-below-zero air.

"She's all set," he grunted, putting the final torque on a bolt with a heavy wrench. "Bring me down and we'll try her out."

Kelln watched with evident pride as the antenna shot swiftly up and down, neatly telescoping into itself each time.

"Nice going," I told Kelln and his radiomen as they gathered their tools to go below. "Now take care of those hands."

I decided to try my luck at some amateur photography, got my camera, and went out on the ice. It was even darker than before and I had to use a light-meter reading to obtain the proper camera setting. If you have ever attempted to work tiny knobs and buttons with heavy gloves on, you know what I was up against. I finally gave up, took off the multilayer mittens, and put them in my pocket. It was marvelous—with ease I could do everything that a few minutes before had been fumbling labor.

I wanted to get a shot of the *Skate* showing the ice that had formed on her sail and superstructure. Water clinging to the metal as it surfaced had frozen instantly when it struck the 20-below-zero air. It gave the ship a gray, glossy sheen which I was trying to catch by light reflection. My absorption with the problem made me forget the cold. Suddenly I noticed that when I turned the knobs of the camera, I couldn't feel a thing. It was as though my fingers didn't exist. The skin had turned a pasty white. I quickly lost interest in photography, buried my hands in my pockets, and ran below decks.

There I found Al Kelln hopping about in pain as the blood circulation slowly began to come back in *his* frost-nipped fingers.

"But I *told* everybody about this!" groaned Dr. Arnest. "Why don't you people *wear* your mittens? That's why the Navy bought them for you."

I told the Doctor that both Kelln and I had nipped our fingers in the performance of highly important work, and would he please restrict himself to curing us and not get out of his field.

The Doctor looked at the frosted camera on my desk and snorted. He poured warm water in my washbasin and said: "Here, soak your hands in this and I guarantee you'll start wearing your mittens."

He was right. As blood—and sensation—began to course through my fingers again, it felt as though each one in turn was being placed on a table and rapped firmly with a hammer. I resolved either to learn to operate my camera with gloves on or give up photography.

This incident drove home to me even more forcibly something I had known all along—our complete inability to care for ourselves in this environment. Soft, unaccustomed to the bitter cold of the arctic winter, we could dash out in it only for short periods; if we were without the warming refuge of the ship for any length of time we would be lost. If the powerful source of nuclear heat throbbing within the heart of the *Skate* should cease to function, this metal cylinder of a ship would quickly succumb to the chill of her surroundings and die. We could never survive—we had no tents, no sledges, no dogs. Infinitely more than last summer, the *Skate* was our lifeline.

CHAPTER 7

After supper we submerged and once more headed for the Pole, now less than 250 miles away. A night of travel under the ice covered the distance and on the morning of the seventeenth we were nearing our destination.

I went over the tape of the ice machine for the preceding hour or so. We were passing under an area of heavily compressed ice with no sign of any we could hope to break. Walt Wittmann was standing by the machine and told me the chances of surfacing near the Pole were slim. Was this place *always* to be our nemesis?

I had not said much to the crew about the service for Sir Hubert Wilkins, mainly because I had become increasingly unsure there would be any. However, this morning I told them over the announcing system what our task was and how we hoped to accomplish it. When we reached the Pole we would start a slow crisscrossing search of the immediate vicinity. If nothing showed up at first, we would be patient and keep searching. The ice cover was constantly shifting, and the new ice coming over might be better. Assuming the ice was moving at 2½ miles a day (an average speed), in twenty-four hours 5000 yards of ice would drift over the North Pole. In that stretch we might be able to find what we wanted.

The test would not be without military value. After we returned from the Arctic in the fall of 1958, many senior officers wanted to know what our chances were of surfacing at a *given* geographic location in the Arctic—not a place like Drift Station Alfa, which shifted with the ice, but an assigned latitude and longitude. Well, we would see.

At the breakfast table the talk was, as usual, of ice. We began discussing the clumsiness of our name for these areas of thin ice which were so vital to us. Actually they were newly frozen leads but that seemed an awkward way to put it. What we needed was a new name. Many were suggested but none seemed to convey the idea. Then Dr. Lyon, who had heard me discussing what they looked like through the periscope, said, "Why don't you just call them skylights?"

And that's what they resembled. They were like a stretch of blue-green translucent glass in an otherwise black ceiling. The places where the ice was thin enough to let in the light to the dark sea below were the places we were looking for to reach the light and air above. *Skylights* they would be.

But we found no skylights as we approached the Pole. We cruised slowly, adjusting our course carefully according to the instructions of Bill Layman. Zane Sandusky and Bob Wadell methodically plotted the readings from their green tubes on reams of orange graph paper. Slowly but surely, the submarine was delicately conned into the spot where every direction is south. The *Skate* had returned to the Pole.

I made a brief announcement to the crew, reminding them of something most of them already knew—that almost exactly fifty years ago (it had been April 6, 1909) Robert Peary had first reached the Pole. How different his circumstances from ours! Accompanied by four Eskimos and his steward, Matt Henson, Peary had had no scientific marvels to guide him to his goal. He measured distance traveled with a crude wheel attached to one of the sledges. His determination of position was by observation of the sun—and this depended partially on a timepiece that had gone for weeks without an accurate check. But Peary had known what he was about. After he had reached the Pole, according to his best navigation, he spent thirty hours marching and countermarching around the general area to make certain he had achieved his goal. He had spent twenty years of his life in its quest and had no desire to miss it by a few miles through miscalculation. When he was certain he had located the Pole as well as his limited equipment would allow, he planted his flags and took his pictures. And then, in a few hours, the drifting ice of the Arctic had carried his flags away from the Pole. The shifting signs of fame!

Our task still lay ahead of us. Thanks to the marvels of inertial navigation, we had reached the Pole with little difficulty. Reaching the surface would be a different matter—that would be up to us.

There was not a sign of a skylight. With the ship stopped 200 feet under the sea directly at the North Pole, I raised the periscope in the hope of seeing something. But the sea was black—absolutely and completely. Not the faintest glimmer shone through the ice above; we were sealed in.

We began our crisscross search in the immediate area, proceeding at very slow speed and using the periscope as well as the ice detector and the television. No luck.

Here at the Pole the sun would still be below the horizon; if the overcast were as heavy as the day before, there wouldn't be much light anyway. Well, I thought, we'd just have to wait and see. Several hours went by with no results.

And then we saw it. At first it was just a faint glimmer of emerald green, visible only through the periscope. It looked too small for the ship, but it was worth investigating. Carefully we maneuvered the *Skate* under it and looked at our ice detector. The trace showed thin ice.

This was a different game from that of last summer, when we made long leisurely loops under lakes, taking care to get ourselves safely in the middle of a relatively large piece of open water. Here, trying to surface at a prechosen spot in winter, we had to be satisfied with a patch of thin ice scarcely large enough to hold us. No need to maneuver the ship beneath it to plot its shape—it was so small we could see the whole area at a glance through the periscope, outlined sharply by the black floes around it. At the same time, we would simply not have had the courage or skill to try such a dangerous and delicate task without the confidence that had come of last summer's experience.

We drifted up to 100 feet. The skylight was dog-legged in shape and treacherously small; we had never attempted anything like this. However, I knew that if we could once break through the ice above us the *Skate* would be held as tightly as in a vise. There would be no danger of damage from drifting into the sides of the small opening.

"Stand by to hit the ice," I said. "Bring her up."

We had barely started up again when Al Kelln, standing at the ice detector, called out nervously, "Heavy ice overhead—better than twelve feet!"

I could see what had happened. The ice was moving, and the skylight was simply drifting away from the submarine.

"Flood her down, Guy!" I said. Reluctantly the three-thousand-ton ship reversed her course and began to sink slowly back into the black depths. Patiently we realigned the ship under the small opening, twisting first one way and then the other with the propellers.

The second try was no better than the first; again we drifted out from under the tiny skylight.

"We'd better try an offset," said Bill. He quickly calculated how far to the side we should position ourselves in order to come up from 100 feet and find ourselves in the right position. Painstakingly the *Skate* was maneuvered into position.

This time, as we started upward, Kelln told us that we had heavy ice overhead. Not a very comfortable feeling, with the top of the sail only 50 feet or so below the ice, but we could only count on the drift to carry us into position.

As we rose, I was forced to lower the periscope. Now we were blind except for the television camera, which showed only the fuzzy edge of the heavy ice.

Now the top of the sail was only 25 feet under the heavy ice. "Heavy ice, still heavy ice," Kelln reported, the strain apparent in his voice. How much longer can we wait?

"Flood her down—emergency!" I snapped. We could wait no longer. The wave of air pressure slapped into my ears as Shaffer opened the vent of the negative tank and sent tons of water cascading into the ship to bring her down. Quickly we fell away from the ominous ice cliffs.

"Blow negative to the mark," Shaffer ordered, trying to regain control of the now swiftly falling *Skate*. The roar of high-pressure air filled the room.

"Blow secured; negative at the mark," reported Chief Dornberg at his side.

"Shut the flood, vent negative, pump from auxiliaries to sea," said Guy, watching his gauges through narrowed eyes.

Slowly our downward momentum slackened and finally, far deeper than we had intended to go, we were once more motionless.

Beads of perspiration were standing out on my brow and I could sense the feeling of strain that ran through the ship. With grim determination, we started all over again.

"There are heavy pressure ridges on either side of this opening except at the dog-leg corner," reported Al Kelln. "I've had a chance to catch them on the ice detector."

Once more Bill Layman calculated the offset required, this time allowing for a little less drift.

I attempted to set the ship near the corner of the dog-leg to avoid the ridges Al had mentioned. The whir of the trimming pump announced our slow ascent.

"Heavy ice, still heavy ice," intoned Kelln like the voice of doom. Time for the periscope to go down.

"Thin ice! There she is! Looks good!" exclaimed Al.

The television screen showed us very close. We braced ourselves. With a sickening lurch we hit and broke through.

"Don't let her drop out, Guy," I warned. Again I had the feeling of having a tenuous foothold at the top of an impossible peak.

Shaffer put a puff of air into the ballast tanks; we seemed to be maintaining our position. I raised the periscope on the chance of seeing something; I was most reluctant to surface blind when I knew heavy pressure ridges were close by.

The periscope went up, but revealed nothing but a field of blank white. Frozen.

I glanced at the diving instruments; we were holding our position well. If we could break through, we would make history.

"Stand by to surface at the Pole," I announced over the speaker system.

Swiftly preparations were made, and Shaffer turned to me with a smile, "Ready to surface," he said, "at the Pole!"

Slowly we blew the tanks and the *Skate* moved reluctantly upward. It was apparent we were under heavier ice here than any we had experienced before. After what seemed an eternity of delay, the upper hatch was far enough above the ice to be opened. Our tenuous foothold was becoming more firm.

"Open the hatch!" I shouted, and raced up the ladder. The ice we had broken was so heavy that it had not fallen into the bridge but had split and fallen outside. I leaped to the bridge and was struck by the first heavy wind I had ever experienced in the Arctic. It howled and swirled across the open bridge, carrying stinging snow particles which cut like flying sand. Heavy gray clouds hung in the sky; the impression was of a dark and stormy twilight about to fade into night.

We had broken through almost exactly at the bend of the dog-leg. The lead was narrow and heavily hummocked on either side, wandering into the blowing snow like a meandering creek for the quarter of a mile or so I could see. These hummocks were the tallest we had yet seen in the Arctic—we later estimated their height at 18 feet.

Although we were closer to one side of the narrow lead than I would have liked, we seemed to have a clear path in which to surface the rest of the way. Only our sail protruded from the ice, but the ship was held tightly—there was no chance of drifting.

The phones were rigged and the tanks blown with high-pressure air. With loud cracks that sounded like gunshots, the deck began to break through. This lead had frozen with many large chunks of heavier ice floating in it. They were now caught in the matrix of the thinner ice like almonds in chocolate.

Finally the *Skate* lay on the surface—the first ship in history to sit at the very top of the world. In every direction—ahead, astern, to port, to starboard—was south. The planet turned ponderously beneath us. When the sun rose on March 19, just two days away, it would swing around the horizon for twenty-four hours in a perpetual sunrise.

The *Skate* had arrived at her goal. Last summer's attainment of the Pole had brought little satisfaction because we had been forced to remain submerged where, for all the difference it made to us, we could have been anywhere else in the oceans of the world. Only our instruments had told us we were there.

But this—with its blowing snow and lowering sky—this was the North Pole. The lodestone of the Arctic, which had lured brave men to their deaths for over a century and which had even been denied to the indomitable Nansen, had fallen to the modern submarine.

Too easily? Would those brave men of fifty years ago have resented our easy conquest? I thought of what Peary had written about his arrival at the Pole. He had attempted to put down in his diary the emotions of the hour, but could not. He was exhausted, and all seemed commonplace. Later he wrote:

If it were possible for a man to arrive at 90 degrees north latitude without being utterly exhausted, body and brain, he would doubtless enjoy a series of unique sensations and reflections ... but the grim guardians of earth's remotest spot will accept no man as guest until he has been tried and tested by the severest ordeal.

CHAPTER 8

After a walk out on the ice, Walt Wittmann warned me that he did not like the looks of our surroundings. There had been heavy ice movement recently, and with the wind (about 30 knots, a stiff gale) blowing as hard as it was, there was every reason to expect more. Walt advised us not to stay any longer than necessary.

We made immediate preparations for the service. Sir Hubert had been born in Australia, had performed many of his finest deeds for the United Kingdom, and had made his final home in the United States. In recognition of this we flew the flags of all three nations from the masts and periscopes of the *Skate*. They made a brave sight snapping sharply in the wind.

We formed a small table on the ice beside the ship from some boxes and covered it over with a green baize cloth. On this we placed the bronze urn. About thirty of the crew formed ranks on either side of the table in the 26-below-zero cold. We were on the port side of the *Skate* and as much in its lee as possible. Our breath froze on our chins and the edges of our hoods and gave us the appearance of having white beards. The wind blew snow into our noses and mouths, and it was difficult to talk or even breathe.

It was too dark to read easily without some sort of light, so men held red flares on both sides of the altarlike table. Their shimmering light glared through the blowing snow, giving the scene unearthly atmosphere. The red glow reached to the three flags crackling above the sail of the ship and made them stand out in the gloom as though they were specially lighted.

The remainder of the crew lined up on the deck of the *Skate* and a rifle squad formed near the bow. The wind and bitter cold made it physically difficult to hold and read the prayer book, but I began:

> I am the resurrection and the life, saith the Lord: he that believeth in me, though he were dead, yet shall he live: and whosoever liveth and believeth in me, shall never die. I know that my redeemer liveth. . . .

In a few words I then tried in my own way to catch the essence of the man: "On this day we pay humble tribute to one of the great men of our century. His indomitable will, his adventurous spirit, his simplicity, and his courage have all set high marks for those of us who follow him. He spent his life in the noblest of callings, the attempt to broaden the horizons of the mind of man.

"Some of his personality is expressed in this prayer which he himself wrote: 'Our heavenly Father, wouldst thou give us liberty without license and the power to do good for mankind with the self-restraint to avoid using that power for self-aggrandizement. . . .' "

Lieutenant Boyd then picked up the bronze urn and, followed by me and the two torchbearers, walked about 30 yards away from the ship. In the lurid glow of the torches, I read the committal:

> Unto Almighty God we commend the soul of our brother departed, and we commit his ashes to the deep; in sure and certain hope of the Resurrection unto eternal life, through our Lord Jesus Christ; at whose coming in glorious majesty to judge the world, the sea shall give up her dead. . . .

Dave took the urn and sprinkled the ashes to the wind. They quickly disappeared in the half-darkness and the swirling snow. The rifles cracked three times in a last salute. Sir Hubert Wilkins had reached his final resting place.

Dinner that evening was a sober gathering—all of us had been touched by the solemn circumstances of the service. It seemed

a tribute not only to Wilkins but to all the men who had spent
their lives in the conquest of the North.

That night we built a small cairn of ice blocks and planted
a steel shaft in it to which we attached an American flag. There
had been much discussion about other flags—those of various
organizations, for instance. We finally decided, however, there
was only one flag we could leave at the North Pole—the flag
of the nation whose power, wealth, and skill had made it possible for us to come.

In a waterproof container buried inside the cairn we left this
note:

17 March 1959

Deposited on this date in a cairn at the geographic North
Pole by the United States Submarine *Skate*.

The *Skate* surfaced at the North Pole on 17 March 1959
and conducted memorial services for the late Sir Hubert
Wilkins.

The return of this container to the commanding officer
of the *Skate* along with notation of the date and location of
recovery will be a contribution to the cause of international
science.

James F. Calvert
Commanding

In due time this message may, like the wreckage of the *Jeannette,* be carried along in the ice drift to be cast up eventually
on the shores of Greenland far to the south.

There had been no sign of the ice movement that Wittmann
had feared, but the gale was increasing and the temperature
dropping. We decided it was time to return to the warmer environment of the sea. It no longer seemed so remarkable to
think of the water of the winter Arctic as warm. Sea water cannot be much colder than 28 degrees Fahrenheit without freezing, and the Polar Sea is about 29 degrees—sixty degrees or so
warmer than the winter air.

For once, the squawk of the diving alarm sounded oddly inappropriate in the warm hush of the ship. The vents opened and we began to sink slowly into the canyon of ice. The wind roared and whipped over the jagged hummocks. The cairn we had made was plainly visible through the periscope a few yards to port. The last thing I saw was the American flag whipping proudly in the swirling, windswept snow.

CHAPTER 9

Early on Thursday the nineteenth we were in uncharted waters deep in eastern longitude and picked up signs of a large skylight. It had been over thirty hours since we had surfaced; and this seemed a fine opportunity to check on conditions in a part of the Arctic in which we had never been before.

Confidently we swung back underneath the skylight; the plotting party went smoothly into action. The estimated elevation and direction of the sun were handed to me on a slip of paper. Through the periscope I could see a faint flush of light from above. The ice looked very similar to that in which we had first surfaced on Sunday.

Our ascent was smooth and expert; on the television we could clearly see the black bulk of the sail near the ice. Then we hit with a jolting crunch stronger than anything we had felt before. We watched the screen expectantly. Nothing happened. It was as though we had come up against solid concrete. We were bouncing away. I cautiously raised the periscope. The glare of the floodlights threw the smooth underside of the ice into sharp relief. We had not left even a mark.

For a long time no one said anything. Finally, I heard a low chuckle nearby.

"Well, Captain," said an amused voice, "at least you're still three for four!" As I might have known, it was Medaglia.

In a way, I was grateful to him for relieving the tension. But we had failed, there was no denying it.

Fortunately, a careful examination of our equipment revealed no damage to the ship. But as we continued on our way we were less sure of ourselves.

Twice more that day we had the same experience—what looked like good skylights proved impossible to break. Our confidence was evaporating. What would we do if we had trouble with the ship now? The answer to that was so plain none of us wanted to think about it.

For the first time on either of the *Skate*'s expeditions, I seriously considered turning back. We were in an area of the ocean where apparently we could not find the thin ice upon which our safety depended. But where *could* we find it? The only sure place was where we had come from—the other side of the North Pole. There was no way of telling what lay ahead of us.

I finally decided to press on. We had had one bad day, but I still hoped the next would bring better luck. During the night the seal around the starboard propeller shaft began to leak again, and although we were able to slow it down to a trickle by backing the shaft once more, this didn't add to anyone's peace of mind.

The next day had anything but an auspicious start. Before breakfast we made two more unsuccessful attempts to break through. We were now more than 1200 nautical miles—greater than the distance from Chicago to Salt Lake City—from open water. It looked like time to turn back. Still reluctant to retreat, I conferred with Walt Wittmann, Dr. Lyon, and the ship's officers in the wardroom.

Walt said that he believed our chances of finding looser ice should improve almost any hour. Lyon essentially agreed. I decided to continue for at least one more day.

And even while we were still sitting in the wardroom we felt the ship heel sharply to starboard as the officer of the deck doubled back to have another look at a possible skylight. I went immediately to the control center and asked how it looked.

"Small, but worth a look," said Bill Cowhill laconically.

In a few minutes I was able to look at the opening through the periscope. We were still keeping Greenwich time, and here, on the other side of the world, night and day were reversed. The sun had set in the morning, and it was now well below the horizon. It would be quite dark above the ice. Even so, I could see a faint emerald streak across our roof of black.

As we attempted to come up we had the same experience as at the Pole—the opening was drifting away from us. As before, we tried to allow for the drift, but this time we could not seem to hit it right. Either we offset too much or not enough.

The lead was long and narrow; the *Skate* was being set across it rather than parallel to its long side. We were able to position the ship diagonally across the lead, and we crabbed it around as best we could as we came up, by reversing one propeller and going ahead on the other.

In the deep gloom, the floodlight on the sail made a brilliant spot on the underside of the ice. Suddenly the light disappeared and all was darkness. For a moment we were baffled. Eventually we realized what had happened—the light was shining up into thin air! We had broken through so easily we had not felt it.

Cheers of triumph and relief rang through the ship when the word went out. Quickly air was released into the tanks, and we were soon at the top of the ladder clearing away the ice on the bridge. It was even darker than I had thought: this had made the ice look thicker than it was. It was, in fact, very thin, which explained why our passage through it had been so easy.

The scene was different from anything we had experienced before. There was not a cloud in a sky brilliant with stars. I have never seen them look so close or so clear. There was a three-quarter moon which, reflected by the snow and ice, gave a surprising amount of light—just as Stefansson had predicted. The gentle breeze over the ice fields felt bitter cold.

The ship was positioned diagonally across the long, narrow lead. The small hummocks lining either side looked like snow plowed off to the sides of a street. The moon cast weird shadows in the jumbled ice, and the fields of sastrugi were accented by black shadows which betrayed pressure ridges. The fantastic moonlit landscape and the cloudless star-filled sky combined to create a scene of fragile beauty.

We obviously had little room to spare at bow or stern, but we were securely fixed in the ice and our position seemed safe. I decided we would remain a while, if only to relieve some of the tensions which had built up during the last two days. I was also anxious to give everyone a chance to see our surroundings—this scenery, I thought, could not be duplicated this side of the moon.

These were the first stars we had ever seen in the Arctic; Bill Layman had a field day taking sights in every direction. He was thus able to fix our position with extreme accuracy—which pleased us all, for we had had no way of checking our instruments since leaving the North Pole.

After supper the sun began to rise. The sky had remained clear, and the sun came up over the horizon as sharp and clear as if a red paper disk were being pushed above the horizon. The icefields became flooded with the vermilion glow, and despite the temperature the air felt brisk and invigorating. That it was 23 degrees below zero seemed not to matter.

I was standing on the stern when I was joined by Dave Boyd. The heavy layer of white rime around his facemask indicated he had already been in the open for some time.

"How about trying out the skindiving here?" he asked nonchalantly.

"Good *night,* Dave!" I exclaimed. "Are you out of your mind? It's twenty-three below!" I said.

He laughed. "Soon's we get in that warm water we'll be fine."

It was a sparkling-clear day; the light was as good as any we were likely to find. This was probably the place to try skindiving if we were going to.

"All right," I said. "Go ahead and get ready. We'll take time out for it." Possibly fearing I would change my mind, he ran off without another word.

What a world we were living in! By our watches it was eight o'clock in the evening, but in these longitudes it was dawn, and the light would become better as the "night" progressed. And, at 23 below zero, the crew was getting ready to go swimming.

So closely did the *Skate* fit into the hole in the ice that we had to break a new hole so the aqualungers could enter the water. Dave, Dick Arnest, the doctor's assistant Dick Brown, and soundman Sam Hall clustered about it in their Martian costumes. The heavy sponge-rubber suits covered all but a small part of their faces, making it hard to tell one from another.

Dr. Lyon, having heard about the diving expedition, was on hand with water-sample bottles. "Just uncork these when you get to proper depth," he told Dave. "I'd like them at ten, twenty, and thirty feet."

Dave nodded his understanding, and shifted the three husky bottles of compressed air mounted on his back. Giving his tender, Jim Brissette, a thumbs-up signal that everything was in order, he stepped off the stern into the water. He bobbed in the ice hole for a moment and then went down. A light line was tied to his waist for safety, and the sight of this cord paying out like a fishline into the small hole was odd indeed.

In a short time Dave reappeared in the hole. He held up one of the water bottles, motioned for another, and soon returned with it as well. Resting on the edge of his ice hole, he pulled the rubber breathing piece from his mouth. "This is *great!*" he shouted enthusiastically. "The water's warm and clear as crystal." I was nonetheless not disposed to join him.

After Dr. Arnest had gone under the ice and returned, Brown and Hall set off together on an attempt to reach a pressure ridge that rimmed our lead. After they had been gone nearly ten minutes I was getting more than a little concerned, when their heads appeared simultaneously in the hole.

I crouched down to talk to them. I noticed how pale and blue they both looked. "You all right?" I asked.

Brown nodded. "Just pooped," he gasped. "We're not in shape for this kind of stuff."

"You get to the pressure ridge?"

"Don't think so," said Sam Hall. "It's hard to tell how far you've gone. At any rate I didn't see anything that looked like what we wanted."

Both Brown and Hall indicated they wanted to rest in the water a bit before attempting to climb out. No doubt about it, they were exhausted.

"How was the light?" I asked.

"Good," answered Brown. "And the water is really clear—we never lost sight of the hull."

"The ice in this lead is really flat," said Hall. "Looks like you're swimming under a glass ceiling."

"Any sign of life?" I asked.

"Coupla jellyfish, nothing else." Brown laughed. "The jellyfish never desert us."

When the two men finally tried to climb out of the water, they needed help to make it. And even while they stood on the deck being helped out of their heavy aqualung rigs, the water absorbed by their spongy suits froze. With every step, as they headed for the warm interior of the ship, they tinkled and crashed with a sound like breaking glass.

By 10:30 P.M.—our time—we reluctantly submerged from our skylight on the other side of the world.

As we drove onward at 400 feet and 16 knots, we began to cross the tracks of several drift expeditions, including that of the *Fram*.

By Sunday morning we had reached a point roughly 100 miles from the New Siberian Islands. Here we took a sharp turn of more than 90 degrees to the right to continue our exploration of the polar basin. We were plotting our route carefully so as to remain well within the international waters of the great ocean we were exploring.

Sunday passed quietly with everyone working hard to bring reports and tables of data up to date. About nine in the evening there was a sharp rap on my door. Dave Boyd popped his head in.

"Captain," he said grimly, "we've developed a pretty serious leak in the engine room. I'd like you to come and have a look at it."

CHAPTER 10

On our way to the engine room, I asked Dave, "Where's this trouble seem to be?"

"It's the starboard circ pump," he explained, "at the seal where the drive shaft enters the pump."

The steam from the boilers of the reactor compartment comes into the engine room of the *Skate* at high pressure. It hisses through the blades of the turbines, expending its energy in making them spin at blinding speeds. The spent and pressureless steam drops into a large condenser where it is chilled back to water, to be returned to the boilers where the cycle starts again. The steam is chilled by sea water, circulated through the condenser in half-inch tubes by a centrifugal pump. The men who work in the engine room simply call it a circ pump.

We hastily clambered down the ladder into the lower level of the engine room. There, illuminated in the beam of a flashlight held by one of Dave's engineers, I could see the faulty seal spraying water in every direction. Water ran across the steel deck plates and into the bilge below us, sprayed up where it spit and sizzled on the bare steam pipes of the air ejector, sprayed out, splashing against the metal doors of an electrical switchboard.

"Isn't there any way we can tighten up on it?" I asked.

Dave shook his head. "This is a new type of seal—there's no way of adjusting it. So far they've always been fine, but we've sure got trouble now."

"Won't you have to shut the condenser down to replace the seal?"

He nodded. But shutting down the condenser would be no

simple task. It would mean that half our turbines would also be shut down, and for technical reasons it was most undesirable for us to operate under the ice without all of our turbines in operation.

"Looks as though we'll have to make this repair on the surface," I said.

"I hate to take this job on at all up here in the ice pack," he replied. "It's really a big one," said Boyd.

Engine-room chief Charles Whitehead had been standing by during our conversation. Boyd turned to him to ask his opinion.

"It's a big job all right," Whitehead said. "We'll have to lift that circ pump motor with chain hoists. I guess it weighs about half a ton. I'd hate to be interrupted in the middle."

"There's a chance the thing will reseat by itself," Dave said dubiously. "They do sometimes."

"It's not the job itself that's the worst of it," Whitehead went on. "It's clearing out everything that's in the way. We've got to move all those lockers," he pointed to a bank just above the motor, "plus these pipes and a lot of wires before we can begin to lift the motor."

"Well, it's a job that we'd ask Electric Boat to do if we were home," said Dave, "but if worst comes to worst we can do it here."

I looked at the huge electric motor sitting on top of the doughnut-shaped pump casing. Water was already starting to splash up into the windings of the motor—a little more of that would ruin the motor and we had no replacement for it.

"All we can do is put a canvas cover around it to keep the water from spraying," said Dave.

"Right," I replied. "And when we find a place to surface we'll decide what to do."

We pressed on at high speed for the rest of the night. The fathometer continued to send out its pulses charting the floor of the ocean so accurately that every valley and hill was apparent. At intervals we would drop down into the depths and then rise in stages, hovering at each level while Dr. Lyon measured the temperature of the water and took samples for analysis. On one of these excursions the variation of pressure on the circ pump seal caused it to reseat perfectly. It didn't leak a drop.

However, neither Dave nor I was convinced the trouble wouldn't reappear.

"You know, we had trouble with one of these things on the way home last fall," said Dave. "It reseated and held for several days—then *flooie!*"

As we were talking, the ship banked sharply to starboard as the officer of the deck turned back for some thin ice. As we moved slowly back under the skylight we could see it easily on the television screen. Apparently the light was fairly good.

As we pumped our way up under our fifth polynya, I could see through the periscope two small black spots on the underside of the thin ice. Suddenly I could make out ripples in them. It was the first open water we had seen on the cruise. The puddles, about 2 feet in diameter, showed that the ice in this lead must be very new.

We passed through easily and found ourselves at one edge of a long, narrow, winding lead that wandered off for miles into the distance. The sky was a burnished turquoise, with the sun a carmine disk at the horizon. The wind was stiff—about 15 knots—and blew snow across the sastrugi in little puffs of white. It was 23 below zero.

Now what to do? Fix the pump or not? We were scheduled to remain in the pack for nearly another week. We had many hundreds of miles to travel, many jobs remaining to be done.

I called the officers together for a brief conference in the wardroom. We talked briefly, and then I said: "We'll take a chance on it. No repair, we'll go on. I believe it'll hold."

It was hard for me to realize that we were operating in the same waters where the unlucky *Jeannette* had finally been sunk almost eighty years before.

It had been many years since I had seen the icicle-decorated stone cross at Annapolis that honors George Washington De Long and the men who were with him. I little thought when I first saw that cross that I would ever see the remote part of the world where those men had so valiantly fought for their lives.

For over twenty months the *Jeannette*'s crew stayed with the ship, desperately trying to save her while the ice floes clawed at her from every direction. They, too, had had pump trouble.

It was only after having been caught in the ice for about four months that they received their first really heavy squeeze. They heard the movement of the ice approaching like a distant roll of thunder and then saw pressure ridges forming before their eyes in the icefields that surrounded the ship. The noise increased as the ice moved closer—a deep rumble occasionally highlighted by the sharp crack of breaking floes. Then arose a heavy grinding as huge pieces of ice began to ride over one another, making a sound like the grate of iron against iron in the intense January cold.

The pressure now began to make itself felt against the wooden ship. She shuddered and trembled like a beast in terror. The oakum squeezed from between her planks, and her beams creaked and bowed. Water began streaming into the hull—unless they could pump it out she would not be long afloat.

The chief engineer, George Melville (later head of the Navy's engineers and one of the designers of Theodore Roosevelt's great white fleet), worked frantically to get up steam to operate the mechanical pumps. Meanwhile, hand pumps were manned in shifts, but the men were barely able to keep up with the inrushing sea. It was absolutely vital to get the steam pump going.

That was far from easy. The engine-room fires had long since been put out and the boiler drained. Since there was no chance of moving the ship it had been decided to conserve the supply of coal as much as possible. Melville immediately had to fill the boiler, build up the fires, and make steam to operate the pump. Fortunately, his boilers did not need chemically pure distilled water (as did the *Skate*); the *Jeannette* used ordinary sea water.

Melville opened the seacock to allow water to run into his boiler. Frozen! All his efforts to run water through the long-frozen valve were in vain. From up on deck he could hear the exhausted cries of the men on the hand pumps. Each team, when it needed relief, would cry, "Spell, O!" and a new team would take over. The cries for relief came more and more frequently. It was obvious they could not keep up much longer with the flooding.

Desperately, Melville had his men unbolt the foot-wide manhole cover at the top of the old boiler. When it was finally removed, the men passed up bucket after bucket of the water already knee-deep in the engine room up to a crewman jammed in the narrow space between the boiler and the engine-room overhead. Slowly, the old boiler began to fill—but not fast enough. The water had risen above their knees and was entering the boiler firebox. Soon the fire would be extinguished, and with it, all hope.

But Melville was not a man to give up easily. In 29-below-zero cold, with the water in the engine room lapping at their hips, he and his men rigged a barrel on a hoist to use as a bailer. With this ingenious device and the redoubled efforts of the men on the hand pumps, the level of the water was kept from rising higher.

Meanwhile enough water had been poured into the boiler to operate it. They hastily rebolted the rusty manhole cover. The needle of the steam-pressure gauge began to move. Melville and his men had continued standing in the icy water with half-frozen feet, nursing the precious fire and warming the steam lines. Finally they were ready to put the steam into the nearly submerged pump. It spluttered and then started to pump. A steady stream of water pulsed up out of the engine room and over the side. The exhausted men on the hand pumps received a permanent "Spell, O!"

The *Jeannette* survived that crisis and many another almost as desperate in the sixteen months she continued to float in the ice pack. Finally, however, all hope of escape was lost. In June 1881, a series of ice pressures crushed the hull of the sturdy old wooden ship; pierced with sharp ice slivers like a whale pierced with harpoons, she sank to the bottom of the sea.

Her thirty-three officers and men made their agonized way 100 miles to the southwest over the summer ice, dragging three heavy wooden boats with them as they went. They were finally able to launch their boats and make their way slowly among the drifting floes. Somehow they reached open water and set sail for the Siberian mainland, nearly 400 miles away across the open sea. The boats became separated en route, and one of them was lost at sea with ten men. De Long's boat reached the head of the Lena River delta, but he and all but two of the thirteen with him perished before they could reach help. Melville's boat landed in the same area, but they never found each other.

All of Melville's men were saved, including a Lieutenant John W. Danenhower, whose yet-unborn son was to play a part in another drama of the Arctic.

De Long's expedition, which had sailed so hopefully from San Francisco in July 1879, ended on the bleak tundras of Siberia in October 1881, a handful of men starving and freezing in the snow. And the *Jeannette?* She still rested at the bottom of the polar sea, not far from where we sped by in the *Skate.*

CHAPTER 11

On Sunday, March 22, about seven in the evening, my telephone buzzed urgently. It was Dave Boyd.

"The circ pump seal has just broken loose again!" he reported. "Much worse this time—spraying water all over the place. We'll have to get up and fix it as soon as we can," he said.

There was no need to go back and look. Dave's tone of voice was explicit enough. I went directly to the control center, where Guy Shaffer was on watch, and explained the emergency to him.

"This ice has been really heavy for hours," said Guy grimly. "No point in doubling back."

An air of tenseness and gloom settled over the control center, as the men on watch silently stared at the ice detector and the television. I thought to myself what a fool I had been not to make the pump repair that morning.

Two hours dragged by. Thirty-two miles of heavy, solid ice without a trace of a gap. Who knows how many openings we narrowly missed, going by them only a few yards to one side or the other?

Reluctantly, I went back to my room. I was not helping matters by standing out there staring at the ice machine and television. There were people on watch to do that, and my presence just made them uneasy.

And then, within an hour, the ship heeled to starboard and began a rapid turn. They'd found something! I immediately returned to the control center where Al Kelln had relieved Guy Shaffer.

"It's a big one!" exclaimed Kelln, with a smile from ear to ear.

I looked at the trace of the ice detector. Sure enough, we had passed under several hundred yards of thin ice. The river of light was strong enough to be clearly visible on the television.

We had practiced our maneuvers over and over to reduce the time required to perform them. Now time was all-important. We were soon under the skylight, ballooning slowly upward. Through the periscope, the now-familiar jade-green river was sharply outlined against the jet-black background of the pack.

At 10:13 P.M. we hit the ice with a heavy impact which brought butterflies to our stomachs. But on the television we could see the ice bow and then shatter. We were through.

The sun was just rising. As I climbed to the bridge I could see its faint glow on the horizon, obscured by clouds. A wind of about 10 knots swept across the ice. We had surfaced almost in the exact center of a long, straight lead, heavily hummocked on our port side. The ice in the lead was smooth and uniform, covered with a light coat of snow, and heavier than any we had yet broken. We came through without damage, but once up, were gripped fast.

The sky was gray and depressing; the temperature was 31 below, the coldest we had yet experienced. The tall pressure ridges to port were made of husky slabs 10 to 12 feet thick. Their green edges showed through the covering snow blanket like emeralds in cotton.

Dave Boyd immediately wanted to know if it was all right to go ahead with the pump repair.

"This looks like a good spot, Dave," I told him. "Let's get on with it. How long do you think it will take?"

"I've just talked it over with Whitehead," he said. "We think about twelve hours."

We had never been on the surface that long at any time this winter, but I saw no reason why we couldn't manage it. After all, we'd been at Alfa the summer before more than twenty-four hours.

I decided to go out to have a look at the heavy ridges to port, and went below to put on my heaviest clothes and gather up my binoculars and camera.

The edges of the rafted ice blocks were sharp, showing that they had recently been broken. The ridge itself was about 15 feet high and stretched for hundreds of yards along the side of the lead. I climbed to the top of a hummock and looked back in the direction from which the *Skate* had come. Nothing but endless icefields stretched to the horizon.

I tried to take a few pictures, but had trouble in the biting cold. My fingers were still sore from their nipping of a week before. They felt as though they had been burned on a hot piece of metal and were slowly healing. They were still painful enough to make buttoning a shirt or tying shoelaces difficult.

We had all been out on the ice enough to have keen respect for what the cold could do. We found no matter how carefully we dressed we had trouble keeping our hands and faces warm. Some of the men had taken to wrapping Turkish towels around the lower part of their faces for protection, but the towels were soon stiff and useless with the frozen condensation of their breath.

In the cold and wind, moreover, there was no way to prevent one's eyes and nose from watering. The water would run down cheeks, nose, and chin—and then freeze. As long as we could return frequently to the ship to thaw out we were all right, but attempting to pick or brush the ice off in the open resulted in removing a little skin with it. A raw place was created which itself froze in a short time.

I frankly do not know how men live in temperatures like these, day after day and week after week with no refuge or protection from the weather. Those who have done it have my heartfelt salute.

When I returned to the ship the engine room rang with the voices of men and the clatter of tools. The starboard condenser and its turbines had been shut down and isolated from the leaky seal. Chief Whitehead was in charge of a group of men who were removing the lockers, wires, and small pipes above the motor. Another group prepared a wire sling and block and tackle to hoist the motor.

In the design of the *Skate,* Admiral Rickover's engineers had spared no effort to ensure that every piece of machinery that might have to be repaired at sea could be reached and hoisted out. An elaborate model of the engine room had been built at the Electric Boat Division, in which every piece of machinery, every pipe, every wire, every fitting had been mocked up life-size in wood. Everything was moved around like furniture in a new living room until Rickover's men and the Electric Boat engineers were sure that nothing was inaccessible. That effort was now paying off for us. To be sure, there were impediments around the motor—a submarine engine room must be too full of pipes and wires to avoid this—but they were all light and could be easily moved by the crew.

There was nothing I could contribute here; my presence just made it harder for them to work. I went forward to my room and tried to settle my nerves by reading.

Shortly after, my phone buzzer rang. "Captain," said Al Kelln in a tense voice, "I'd like to have you come up here."

I pulled myself into my warm clothes and climbed to the bridge. As I neared the top of the ladder I could hear a dull boom like distant thunder.

"What's up, Al?" I asked.

In his calm, deliberate manner he handed me his binoculars. "Look over to port," he said, "in the icefields beyond the hummocks."

In the distant icefields, moving with ponderous slowness, huge ice cakes rose up on end like giant green billboards, then slowly slipped back into the surrounding white. The dull thunderous boom grew louder. The ice was on the move.

I looked at my watch. It was 11:25 P.M. The engine-room job had been under way for about an hour. Next to the ship there was still no sign of movement or pressure.

From close to the ship came a noise like the sharp report of a rifle. Startled, I spun around, but could see nothing. Kelln pointed to the bow, where a new crack ran diagonally forward.

Where was the pressure coming from? The wind, although brisk, didn't seem strong enough to cause all this commotion.

I knew, however, that the closely packed ice floes, stretching to the horizon, could transmit pressure from far away. Somewhere, gigantic forces must have been at work to tumble 10-foot blocks of ice like a child's building blocks.

I looked at the fields to port. Now the rise and fall of the ice blocks gave the appearance of sluggish waves, all moving inexorably toward the *Skate.*

As the noise of the grinding, tortured ice grew louder, the ice in the lead started to creep slowly up the sides of the ship. Pieces of it caught on protruding parts of the superstructure, screeching like banshees as they forced their way past the protesting metal.

I could hardly believe what I saw. This was the fifteenth time we had surfaced in the Arctic Ocean and also the first we couldn't submerge easily and quickly.

"Is anyone out on the ice?" I asked.

"I got them down below before I called you," Al answered.

We were all on board and ready to leave this treacherous place—except that we were one hour into a twelve-hour repair job.

"Permission to come up?" It was Bill Layman and Walt Wittmann. I waved them up.

"This pressure is making an awful racket inside the ship," said Bill in a worried tone. "I wanted to see what it looked like."

By now the ice had been forced up over the deck far enough to cover most of the hull. With binoculars, Wittmann studied the ice beyond the steep hummocks to port. "That's mean-looking stuff," he commented. "Can you get out of here?"

I shook my head. "Not now, Walt. Do you think it will stop?"

"You just can't tell with this sort of thing," he said cautiously. "I sure don't see any signs of it stopping."

The pressure ridge that formed on our left was now at least 10 yards closer than when we had surfaced. The lead ice screamed as it was crushed between the moving field on one side and the still-unmoved ice on the other. The lead was clos-ing, and when it did the *Skate* would be caught between the two heavy floes that formed its boundaries, like a walnut in a cracker.

The noise was terrifying. The heavy boom of the moving floes mingled with the high-pitched shriek of the ice in the lead to form an overpowering wall of noise. We all had to shout to make ourselves heard.

I asked Bill Layman to go below to get me a report on the pump repair. The ice of the lead was now being forced up over the deck from both sides, forming a tent-shaped canopy along its length.

From behind the ridge to port a huge blue-green slab of ice rose slowly on edge and hovered ominously as though poised to strike. It was not more than 30 yards away. The noises increased in intensity. Some sounded like the scream of a woman in agony, others like the low-pitched whistle of a night train.

Bill Layman came back to the bridge and told me that the men in the engine room were just ready to hoist the big circ pump motor. Everything was disconnected and nothing secured for motion. The time was 11:35.

"The noise is pretty bad inside the ship, Captain," said Lay-man. "I think you ought to go down and listen to it."

My mouth feeling dry as cotton, I went down the ladder to the control center. I immediately discovered what Layman had meant. The noise of the ice scraping against the thin metal shell of the ship was immensely amplified, sounding as if we were in a steel barrel being dragged along a rock road. Even more dis-turbing than the noise was the vibration. The ship fluttered and shook as the ice pressed around her. She seemed to be protesting the agony she felt.

With a convulsive shudder, she suddenly took an alarming list to starboard. There was no more room for delay. We would have to dive. I was deeply worried about whether the ice might be pressed so tightly against the sides of the ship that she could not submerge. I ran to the engine room. With the noise and vi-bration of the ice pounding about them, men bare to the waist toiled with astounding haste. For an instant, my mind flashed back to Melville and his crew working frantically in the engine room of the *Jeannette.*

I beckoned to Dave Boyd. "I've made up my mind," I told him. "We have to go down. Secure things as quickly as you can and let me know when you're ready."

Dave nodded taciturnly, and turned to his men to order them to undo what they had done. I started back to the bridge, but even as I walked forward into the control center, the noise of the ice against the hull diminished. By the time I mounted the ladder to the bridge it had almost stopped.

"It just stopped," Al Kelln said. "All of a sudden."

The narrow lead in which we lay was now about half its original width, and the ice that filled it was tumbled crazily in every direction, some of it spilled over into the icefield to starboard and much of it rafted like a collapsed house of cards.

"It's going to start again in a moment," Wittmann said, looking out to port with his binoculars. "The ice out there is still moving."

In a few minutes, building up like the climax of music composed in hell, the moaning and screeching reached an even higher level than before. The throbbing vibration could be felt through the deckplates of the bridge. The ice all around the *Skate* was in slow movement, all the more awesome in its deliberate ponderousness. The fragile rudder was buried under a pile of rafted ice and could not be seen.

Everything that I had read and heard about ships trapped in the ice went swiftly through my mind. The *Jeannette,* in these very waters; the *Karluk* of Stefansson, lost in the pressure near Wrangel Island; the *Endurance* of Ernest Shackleton, lost in the Antarctic—all of these had fought the ice and lost. The accounts by their captains of the ice which destroyed them had a striking similarity to what we were now seeing. We would not feel the real crush of the ice until the two heavy floes we rested between were forced together—but I dared not wait for that. The men of the *Jeannette, Karluk,* and *Endurance* had waited beside their crafts, stores and sledges and dogs already evacuated to the ice as the ships went through their death agonies. Their crews had, with great hardship in each case, made their way to land. But we could never do that—our safety lay only in the ship.

In a few minutes Dave Boyd stuck his head up through the hatch to report that the engine room was well enough secured to submerge. They had worked even faster than I had expected. We had only half our engineering plant; we would have to accept the risks and complications involved in operating under the ice this way.

Everyone but Al Kelln hurried below. I shouted to him to come down as soon as he had checked everything for diving.

A circle of gray, tense faces greeted me at the bottom of the ladder. I went to the periscope stand to wait for Kelln to shut the hatch and come down. Why was he taking so long?

The scraping and pounding on the sides of the ship had diminished again, but that did not interest me now. Having made the decision to go, I wanted to go.

"Captain, pick up the phone, please," grated the intercom from the bridge.

I snatched up the phone and said irritably: "What's the delay? Let's go!"

"There's not a sound up here. Not a sign of ice movement. Wish you'd come up and take a look," Al said quickly and a little apologetically.

Nothing is worse on a ship in danger than a captain who vacillates. A bad decision made and stuck to is usually better than indecision. Nevertheless, I put the phone down and went back to the bridge.

The silence was deep and complete. Not a sound could be heard. Was it a temporary respite? I looked at my watch: it was 11:55. It seemed that the pressure had started an eternity ago, but it had been only a little more than half an hour.

I decided to wait, unavoidably keeping one hundred men below in an agony of suspense. Ten minutes went by. I asked Wittmann to come to the bridge. He looked at the ice carefully and said nothing. Anxiously all three of us scanned the icefields beyond the pressure ridge for any sign of movement. None.

About 12:20, a sudden crash of noise nearby convinced me it was starting again, but this time it was the easing of pressure. We suddenly recovered from our list and floated naturally. A few inches of water were visible along the bow.

Now what to do? To hold up diving was one thing, but to begin the job in the engine room and have it again interrupted was another. I debated with myself silently for a few minutes, then leaned over and called down the hatch for Dave Boyd to come to the bridge.

When he arrived I told him to start the pump repair again. I frankly expected at least a mild argument in favor of waiting a bit longer. But all Dave said was a quick, "Aye, aye, sir," and he was on his way. This demonstration of trust and confidence bolstered me more than anything that happened during the whole nightmarish episode.

I resolved to stay on the bridge and watch the ice myself. Illogically, I felt that by my very presence I could prevent the ice from moving again. As the hours crept by with no further sign of ice movement, logic gradually got the better of superstition and I began to see the foolishness of what I was doing. It would be important for me to be fresh in the morning when many of my officers would be half-dead of exhaustion.

I went below to my room and, after taking off my heavy clothes, lay down on my bunk to rest. The nervous tension of the past few hours seemed to ebb away. I fell asleep before I could turn my light off.

I was awakened when Dave knocked on my door. It was six-thirty in the morning. Dave looked exhausted, his eyes bloodshot and his face haggard.

"Repair completed. Ready to submerge, sir."

The job had been done in less than seven hours.

CHAPTER 12

O Eternal Lord God, who alone spreadest out the heavens, and rulest the raging of the sea; Vouchsafe to take into thy almighty and most gracious protection our country's Navy, and all who serve therein. Preserve them from the dangers of the sea. . . .

A small group was assembled for evening prayer in the mess hall of the *Skate*. The day was Sunday, the twenty-ninth of March, exactly a week after our experience with the moving ice. During that week we had continued our explorations: four more surfacings had been accomplished and we had ranged far and wide through the eastern half of the polar sea.

Bruce Meader had finally gotten pictures of the ship coming up through the ice. We had marooned him once more on the floes; and this time he had kept his cameras wrapped in oven-heated blankets and had gotten some excellent pictures. Even the skindivers had had another swim and had come back, blue but happy, with tales of stalactites 6 feet long hanging down under the ice of the lead. Dave Boyd even broke one off and cast it up for us like some treasure from the deep.

We had become more expert at finding thin ice, and never again butted our sail fruitlessly against it. Nor did we ever again see the ice on the move, although we did surface in one place where there were violent traces of recent pressure. Once the temperature was recorded at 41 degrees below zero—our low for the winter.

On Friday the twenty-seventh we passed Prins Karls Forland on the way out of the pack and headed for New London. We sent a message to the Navy Department describing our results briefly. We knew that it had gotten through, because we had been hearing the story of the *Skate* in the news broadcasts each time we came to periscope depth.

Gracious messages of congratulation began coming in. One of the shortest arrived first. It said simply:

WELL DONE X ARLEIGH BURKE

And indeed we had the sense of a job well done. We had been successful beyond our fondest hopes. We had been pioneers in what we knew would be an ocean of destiny.

Indeed, we left the Arctic with deep regret. The first time we surfaced outside the ice pack marked the end of a great adventure, the end of a supreme effort to which we had all given at least two years of our lives. Now it was over; now we were going home. The members of the team would disperse to go their separate ways—not only the Navy crew, but also the dedicated band of civilians—men such as Walt Wittmann, Waldo Lyon, Zane Sandusky, and Cramer Bacque—who had become shipmates in the truest sense of the word.

I personally regretted even more the breakup of the crew. On arrival back home there would be many changes—Layman, Cowhill, Arnest, Shaffer, and many others of our most experienced crewmen would be leaving to join the crews of new nuclear submarines still being built. The *Skate* would never be the same without these men, for in a very real sense they *were* the *Skate*.

In the past year they had faced many dangers; perhaps most difficult of all, they had faced the unknown and made it the familiar. The dark ocean forever covered by its frozen sheath of ice had become their element. They had learned many of its secrets, its perils, its uses; they had learned to love its austere beauty. They had been the tremendous outsiders.

Machinery and instruments had been their sword and shield; without the ingenious and intricate devices of an age of technology they could never have hoped to succeed. But it was not the machines that won the victory; it was the men. To watch them rise to the challenge of the unknown, meeting and solving new problems daily, fulfilling and even surpassing my belief in them, had been one of the finest experiences I had ever had. Their triumph particularly encouraged me because I have always believed that the men who serve in the Navy simply reflect the nation as a whole. I have never felt that Navy men are a special breed; the crew of the *Skate* came from almost every state in the union, from both city and country, from all walks of life. They represented their country in every sense of the word, and their achievements strengthened my confidence and pride in the nation that produced them.

We would always be bound together by the special bond that grows between men who have known danger together. We felt that bond strongly now, reinforced by the spiritual bond of common aspiration for ideals less tangible but even more real. Our feelings were expressed in the words of exultation and thanksgiving which ended the service:

> Lord, now lettest thou thy servant depart in peace, according to thy word.
> For mine eyes have seen thy salvation. . . .

PERSONNEL IN THE USS SKATE DURING THE FIRST POLAR CRUISE, AUGUST 1958

OFFICERS

Richard T. Arnest
George A. Barunas, Jr.
David S. Boyd

James F. Calvert
William J. Cowhill
Pat M. Garner
Albert L. Kelln

William H. Layman
John H. Nicholson
Guy H. B. Shaffer

ENLISTED MEN

Bozzel F. Adkins
George T. Albrecht
Donald R. Andrews
Raymond L. Aten
William G. Barber
Phillip E. Batson
Ronald B. Beyer
Joe L. Brackney
William H. Bradley
Edward Briggs
James A. Brissette
Richard F. Brown
Julian R. Buckley
Alden K. Bugbee
William C. Burns
Walter J. Bydairk
Donald L. Campbell
Gilbert C. Carter
Earl F. Conlogue
Theodore G. Dick
Norman R. Dickinson
Paul G. Dornberg
John T. Elliott
Norman P. Eltringham
Alfred C. Emunson
Bernerd J. Flanagan
William R. Gardner
Lawrence D. German
Marquis C. Gibbs

Orman A. Graham
Roger W. Greenough
Joseph W. Haley
James E. Hester
Clarence Hobbs
Harold J. Hubble
Frank D. Imlay
Ralph T. Jacobs
Woodrow W. Jones
Valery C. Keaveny
Aubrey F. King
James G. Kippen
William B. Kirkendall
Robert W. Kittle
Louis E. Kleinlein
Charles A. Lasch
Robert E. Law
Harold J. Lien
Alexander J. Martin
Dale L. McCord
John F. Medaglia
Ray Meadows
David H. Mitchell
John H. Morrissey
Robert K. Moyle
Charles H. Mullen
Donald E. Nault
Donald E. Nelson
Frederick O'Brien
Adrien A. Paquette

Cletus E. Qualls
James J. Regan, Jr.
Mario M.
    Ressurreccion
Gordon E. Rouiller
Wayne Rouse
Duane M. Sanger
Louis F. Schuman
David L. Seymour
Jerome V. Smith
William D. Spoon
Fred R. Stafford
John W. Stoffel
Albert E. Strong
Phillip C. Stryker, Jr.
Melvin M. Surdel
Jerry I. Taylor
Kenneth N. Taylor
John W. Turner
James E. Van Doren
Teddy G. Vaughn
Elton D. Wallander
Clarence E. Warren
Otto H. Welper
Charles T. Whitehead
Arthur G. Williams
Paul R. Williams
Wayne L. Winans
Erwin C. Young

CIVILIAN SCIENTISTS AND TECHNICIANS

Eugene C. LaFond
Arthur E. Molloy
Rexford N. Rowray

Zane A. Sandusky
David C. Scull
Clark Ingraham

Roger E. Schmidt
Walter Wittmann
Francis G. Weigle

SECOND POLAR CRUISE, MARCH 1959

OFFICERS

Richard T. Arnest
George A. Barunas, Jr.
David S. Boyd
Richard J. Boyle

James F. Calvert
William J. Cowhill
Pat M. Garner

Albert L. Kelln
William H. Layman
Bruce I. Meader
Guy H. B. Shaffer

ENLISTED MEN

Donald R. Andrews
Theodore A.
    Archambault
Douglas C. Armstrong
Raymond L. Aten
Phillip E. Batson
Charles B. Bergland
Pete Bertram
Ronald B. Beyer
George R. Bible
Joe L. Brackney
William H. Bradley
James A. Brissette
Richard F. Brown
Julian R. Buckley
William C. Burns
Donald L. Campbell
Newell E. Carson
Joseph D. Conner
Theodore G. Dick
Paul G. Dornberg
Alfred C. Emunson
Bernerd J. Flanagan
Raymond A. Fritz
Raymond T. Gay
Lawrence D. German
Orman A. Graham
James N. Hall
James E. Hester
Clarence Hobbs

Frederick R.
    Hollendonner
Harold J. Hubble
Frank D. Imlay
Ralph T. Jacobs
Woodrow W. Jones
Valery C. Keaveny
James G. Kippen
William B. Kirkendall
John F. Kirkpatrick
Louis E. Kleinlein
Charles A. Lasch
Harold J. Lien
Lawrence L. Loring
Archie L. Lusk
Lawrence A. Mapes
Alexander J. Martin
Elam L. Mauk
Robert P. Maynard
Dale L. McCord
John F. Medaglia
David H. Mitchell
Robert K. Moyle
Charles H. Mullen
Aubin Mura
Donald E. Nault
William S. Neill
Donald E. Nelson
Harold D. Nuckols
James H. Norris

Frederick O'Brien
Bruce G. Pardee
Cletus E. Qualls
Rolando C. Reyes
Joseph J. Ring
Gordon E. Rouiller
Wayne Rouse
Duane M. Sanger
Roger W. Schlief
Louis F. Schuman
David L. Seymour
William D. Spoon
John W. Stoffel
Albert E. Strong
Phillip C. Stryker, Jr.
Melvin M. Surdel
Jerry I. Taylor
Kenneth N. Taylor
Arnold W. Toivonen
Philip D. Trowbridge
John W. Turner
James E. Van Doren
Elton D. Wallander
Clarence E. Warren
Otto H. Welper
Charles T. Whitehead
Arthur G. Williams
Paul R. Williams
Wayne L. Winans
Erwin C. Young

CIVILIAN SCIENTISTS AND TECHNICIANS

Cramer D. Bacque
Waldo K. Lyon
Robert L. Merton

Zane A. Sandusky
W. E. Schatzberg

David C. Scull
Robert E. Wadell
Walter Wittmann

INDEX

Adkins, Bozzel F., 120, 213
Albrecht, George T., 213
Alfa, Drifting Ice Station, 85–87, 91, 97–99, 101, 103, 106–108, 139, 153, 177
  described, 112–116
  history of, 110–111
  Skate visits, 109–121
Algae, 125
Amundsen, Roald, 64, 139
Anderson, Cmdr. William, 58–59
Andrews, Donald R., 213, 214
Antarctica, 22–23, 136, 138
Archambault, Theodore A., 214
Armstrong, Douglas C., 214
Arctic, average temperatures, 28, 73
  first submarines into, 22; *see also* Nautilus
  "heat budget" of, 113
  Institute of the (Leningrad), 145
  literature of, Stefansson collection (Dartmouth), 145
  silence, 104
  summer characteristics, 78, 115, 124, 127, 139
  water, 3, 88, 99, 128, 186
  winter characteristics, 124, 144, 147–148
Arctic Circle, 157
Arctic Ocean, size of, 54
  strategic location of, 20–21
Arnest, Richard T., 42, 153, 154, 169, 176, 192, 210, 213, 214
Assur, Dr. Arthur, 116, 121
Aten, Raymond L., 45–47, 125, 213, 214
Atomic Energy Commission, 12, 16, 17

Atomic pile, *Skate*'s, 36–38, 83
Auroras, 115–116

Bacque, Cramer D., 152–153, 171, 210, 214
Baker Memorial Library (Dartmouth), arctic collection, 145
Banks Island, 25, 148
Barber, William G., 213
Barunas, George A., Jr., 213, 214
Batson, Phillip E., 213, 214
Bendix Corporation, 152
Bergen, Norway, 131–133, 139, 141, 143
Bergland, Charles B., 214
Bertram, Pete, 214
Bettis Atomic Laboratory, 79
Beyer, Ronald B., 213, 214
Bible, George R., 214
Bilotta, Maj. Joseph (USAF), 109–112, 117, 118, 120
Blue Dolphin, 145
Boarfish, 23
Bolitho, William, 105
Book of Common Prayer, 75, 185, 209, 211
Boundary, ice, 56, 65, 131, 160
Boyd, David S., 31–35, 64, 87, 98, 99, 122, 123, 152–154, 160, 161, 169, 185, 191–196, 200, 201, 206–209, 213, 214
Boyle, Richard J., 156, 214
Brackney, Joe L., 213, 214
Bradley, William H., 213, 214
Bravo, Drifting Ice Station, 86
Briggs, Edward, 213
Brissette, James A., 89, 90, 192, 213, 214

ABOUT THE AUTHOR

James Calvert is a native of Ohio, and grew up in the small town of Berlin Heights, near Cleveland. He attended Oberlin College and then entered the U.S. Naval Academy, from which he graduated in 1942. He served as executive officer of the submarine *Jack* during World War II, and was twice awarded Silver Star and Bronze Star medals. Following the war he commanded the submarine *Trigger* and then was selected for training in atomic submarines. In recognition of his achievements in polar exploration with the USS *Skate* he was twice awarded the Legion of Merit, and the *Skate* won two Navy Unit Commendations. He later commanded Submarine Division 102, which included the celebrated nuclear submarines *Skate*, *Nautilus*, *Seawolf*, *Skipjack*, and *Triton*. His home is in St. Michaels, Maryland.

The **Naval Institute Press** is the book-publishing arm of the U.S. Naval Institute, a private, nonprofit society for sea service professionals and others who share an interest in naval and maritime affairs. Established in 1873 at the U.S. Naval Academy in Annapolis, Maryland, where its offices remain today, the Naval Institute has more than 85,000 members worldwide.

Members of the Naval Institute receive the influential monthly magazine *Proceedings* and discounts on fine nautical prints, ship and aircraft photos, and subscriptions to the bimonthly *Naval History* magazine. They also have access to the transcripts of the Institute's Oral History Program and get discounted admission to any of the Institute-sponsored seminars offered around the country.

The Naval Institute's book-publishing program, begun in 1898 with basic guides to naval practices, has broadened its scope in recent years to include books of more general interest. Now the Naval Institute Press publishes more than seventy titles each year, ranging from how-to books on boating and navigation to battle histories, biographies, ship and aircraft guides, and novels. Institute members receive discounts of 20 to 50 percent on the Press's nearly 600 books in print.

Full-time students are eligible for special half-price membership rates. Life memberships are also available.

For a free catalog describing Naval Institute Press books currently available, and for further information about U.S. Naval institute membership, please write to:

Membership & Communications Department
U.S. Naval Institute
118 Maryland Avenue
Annapolis, Maryland 21402-5035
Telephone: (800) 233-8764
Fax: (410) 269-7940